EYES ON CULTURE

*Multiply Excellence
in Your School*

Emily Paschall

ConnectEDD Publishing

Chicago, Illinois

Praise for
Multiply Excellence in Your School

Culture touches every corner and paints each wall within a school. *Eyes on Culture: Multiply Excellence in Your School* pushes us as educators, parents, and advocates for children to consider how we are doing our part to actively contribute and cultivate excellence in our school. Emily combines a thoughtful collection of personal anecdotes, actionable ideas, and reflective questions that the reader can use to make important cultural shifts. By the end, you are left with a toolbox of inspiration and motivation to plant seeds for a school culture that roots itself in making school an exciting, safe, and inclusive place for all stakeholders to be.

—**Adam Dovico,** educator and author of *When Kids Lead,*
The Limitless School, and *Inside the Trenches*

In *Eyes on Culture: Multiply Excellence in Your School,* Emily offers clear and powerful stories that will bring about the much-needed development of culture in our schools today. With strategies and simple ideas to get you started, or to the next level of multiplying the excellence with your students and staff. This book is sure to resonate with educators everywhere and I know you'll love the passion and excitement that Emily brings to her work with students and staff on a daily basis. Get your eyes on that school culture, it's more important than ever!

—**Adam Welcome,** educator, author, speaker

Emily makes a strong case for educators to be thermostat adjusters, not temperature readers. Filled with vulnerability, I admire Emily for her transparent, on-the-ground stories. She demonstrates how school climate is measured and adjusted by the collaboration and responsibility of all stakeholders while making the claim that we have the ability to shape the temperature of opinion. Emily articulately describes how to shift the minds of others within school culture to allow students to flourish as they should.

—**Brian Aspinall,** educator, author & CEO Code Breaker Inc.

In *Eyes on Culture: Multiply Excellence in Your School,* Emily Paschall shares her passion for education and her mission, that all educators can make a positive impact within their schools each and every day. This book is infused with stories, lessons, and ideas that will encourage, inspire, and motivate you as you continue your educational journey.

—**Jonathan W. Alsheimer,** Teacher, Speaker, and Author of *Next-Level Teaching*

In *Eyes on Culture: Multiply Excellence in Your School,* Emily Paschall takes you on an inspiring journey through personal stories, reflective questions, and unique culture builders. I connected to the heart in every story and learned new strategies educators can use to build and grow relationships where everyone is valued. Paschall shares how you can enhance the culture by multiplying relentless passion for kids, exemplary instruction in classrooms, and support systems for all teachers. I highly recommend this book as a must-read for anyone ready to create a dynamic school culture as you discover your WHY as an educator.

—**Barbara Bray,** Speaker, Podcast Host, Author of *Define Your WHY*

Emily is a force to be reckoned with. She is full of light and energy and throughout the book I found myself getting more and more excited about the takeaways I would be able to immediately implement. With the importance of culture building (in any workplace), this book is one you must add to your professional library immediately.

—**Todd Nesloney,** Director of Culture & Strategic Leadership for TEPSA

There is no better time than now to double down on our investment in school culture. Afterall, the wellbeing of our staff and students will ultimately lead to the wellbeing of our communities. Emily Paschall gives sage advice in *Eyes on Culture: Multiply Excellence in Your School* by illustrating how it is not the grandiose gestures and meticulously planned events that lead to a strong culture. Rather, it is the cumulation of each of our intentions, mindsets, and interactions over time that ultimately makes school a place in which humans grow and thrive.

—**Amy Fast,** principal, McMinnville High School

Emily shines a light on the secrets to a healthy school culture and positive relationships with students. Her words will speak to the heart of educators and remind school leaders what matters most in our schools. Her stories will leave you feeling connected and validated, while providing you authentic ways to cultivate positive interactions with everyone in your school. This book challenges us all to be more for others and allow others to invest in us.

—**Bethany Hill,** teacher, administrator

Paschall absolutely nails it with tangible ideas and ways to connect with your school community. She understands the needs of our students and shifts the focus to connections, relationships, and excellence.

—**Lindsey Howe,** elementary school administrator, MA

If you want to achieve excellence in your school, a multi-action approach is needed. Emily has gifted us with the perfect playbook that builds hope, deepens a growth mindset and inspires positive behavior of teachers and students alike so excellence becomes the norm for schools and not the exception.

—**Marlena Gross-Taylor,** social commerce entrepreneur, founder of EduGladiators, author, speaker

In *Eyes on Culture: Multiply Excellence in Your School,* Emily Paschall engages the reader on an amazing journey using personal stories, proactive resources, effective questions, and impactful culture builders. From beginning to end, the reader is able to add effective ideas on positive culture building to his or her toolbox. Teachers, coaches, and administrators will be well-served by reading this book. I highly recommend this book to anyone ready to have a positive impact on culture and anyone ready to grow as a person and leader.

—**Vic Wilson,** executive director, council for leaders in Alabama schools

It's no secret that leadership and school culture lay the foundation of success in today's schools. Yet in many places, toxicity is real, as egos, pride, and a me-first attitude reign supreme. In *Eyes on Culture: Multiply Excellence in Your School,* Paschall will reignite your passion, re-center your purpose, and walk by your side to help you be the merchant of hope that those you lead so desperately need. Her stories, practical ideas, and resources will help guide your personal journey forward, as they did mine.

—**Thomas C. Murray,** director of innovation, Future Ready Schools®, author of *Personal & Authentic: Designing Learning Experiences that Impact a Lifetime*

Emily Paschall does a fantastic job of bringing the core principles of school culture to life. The messages are woven into stories that are relatable to all school leaders. You may not know Olivia, Chloe, or Jeremy but you all have someone in your school that matches the need to have their story told. *Eyes on Culture: Multiply Excellence in Your School* will not only help you with the process to develop a systematic approach to raising the level of your team, but it will also inspire you to wake up, walk the walk, talk the talk, and build a team of excellence.

—**Joe Sanfelippo, PhD.,** superintendent, author

Wow! I am blown away! Not only does Emily take us on an incredible journey through her many years, and many roles, in education, but she has packed this book full of actionable takeaways that you can put in place TODAY to make the culture of your classroom, school, and community BETTER. Emily is vulnerable, sharing the countless lessons she has learned along the way. But she is also strategic about how she tells these stories, transforming this book into a guide we can all use to truly multiply excellent culture in our schools. I can't think of a better way to kick off ConnectEDD's *Eyes on Culture* series. Go on this journey with Emily. Find hope, get inspired, take action, create change, build culture, and be better for your kids every day.

—**Jeff Gargas,** COO / Co-founder, Teach Better Team

This publication is available at discount pricing when purchased in quantity for educational purposes, promotions, or fundraisers. For inquiries and details, contact the publisher at: info@connecteddpublishing.com

Published by ConnectEDD Publishing LLC
Chicago, IL
www.connecteddpublishing.com

Cover Design: Kheila Dunkerly

Eyes on Culture: Multiply Excellence in Your School/ Emily Paschall. — 1st ed.
Paperback ISBN: 978-1-7348908-2-2
Ebook ISBN: 978-1-7348908-3-9

EYES ON CULTURE

Multiply Excellence in Your School

TABLE OF CONTENTS

DEDICATION

I dedicate this book to every one of my students, past, present, and future: You are the best teachers I have ever had. Thank you for playing the greatest role in shaping me into the educator I am today.

Foreword

In 2017, Jimmy Casas published *Culturize: Every Student. Every Day. Whatever It Takes.*, which quickly became one of the bestselling education books of the modern era. In addition, since writing *Culturize*, Casas has spoken to thousands of educators around the country, elaborating on central themes of the book and providing strategies for enacting practices in schools and districts everywhere designed to achieve the types of schools we need for our children in the 21st century. The four core "Culturize" principles Casas writes and speaks about are simple, yet profound: As educators, we must (1) Champion for Students (2) Expect Excellence (3) Carry the Banner and (4) Be a Merchant of Hope. However, it is not enough that individual educators exhibit these behaviors; instead, we must create cultures in which all school community members are dedicated to these four core principles. Creating a culture of kind, caring, honest, and compassionate educators designed to challenge and inspire each member of the school community to become more than they ever thought possible is the overarching intent behind the *Culturize* philosophy.

In addition to the thousands of educators who have heard Casas speak and who have read his books, many schools and districts have also conducted book studies based on *Culturize*. As a result, in 2020, ConnectEDD Publishing created a *Culturize Action Guide* to serve as a resource for educators embarking on such book studies. The *Action Guide* is designed to serve as a road map to taking specific action steps as a school community based on the ideas found in *Culturize*. However, perhaps the most rewarding response from educators who have read and been inspired by the book has come from those who have shared their stories of taking the principles from *Culturize* and incorporating them into their own classrooms, schools, and districts. Many teachers, principals, and district office leaders have shared stories so powerful that we decided to ask them to formalize these stories in book format and the idea for a limited series of books based on *Culturize* was born.

In thinking of a title for this series, we started with the premise that the focus of *Culturize* is, of course, "culture," and that we should constantly be "looking at" and examining our current culture juxtaposed with our desired culture and doing everything we can to close the gap from "status quo" to "desired status." And, just as we often need "all hands on deck" when it comes to the work we do, we also need "all eyes on culture" when it comes to ensuring excellence throughout our schools and districts; thus, the series, *Eyes on Culture*. The book you are about to read is the first in this series and we could not be more proud to kick it off with a focus on culture at the school level written by one of the most genuine and passionate elementary school educators we know, Emily Paschall. In *Multiply Excellence in Your School*, Emily shares not only her own journey as an educator, but also a thoughtful journey others can take to "culturize" their classroom, school, or district so that students and staff achieve their true potential. Thank you for reading *Multiply Excellence in Your School* and sharing your thoughts. We hope this book motivates and inspires educators to do whatever it takes to ensure a culture of excellence in every classroom and every school. If we can assist in any way with the work you are doing, please reach out to us at:

ConnectEDDPublishing (563) 447-5776 or
info@connecteddpublishing.com

Please also share your thoughts, along with the work you are doing related to this book, via social media using the hashtag *#MultiplyExcellence*. Thank you for your dedication and commitment to excellence and to the students we serve.

Introduction

I recently read a statistic on a Twitter post which said that fewer than 50% of students believed they had a teacher who cared about them as an individual.

When I read this, it punched me right in the gut. How have we failed so many kids? I think we can all agree that we did not go into education for the money. We chose education because we are moved by passion in the classroom, progress in students, and improving futures.

So, what are we missing? Why do over half our students feel that we do not care about them?

As educators, it is easy to get discouraged by all that we are asked to accomplish each day. We wear the hat of teacher, counselor, nurse, social worker, cheerleader—the list is endless. We feel pressured by a system or program, and if we are not careful, these pressures can easily suck the joy out of what we get to do each day—emphasis on: GET to do.

We **get** to make learning fun.
We **get** to improve kids' futures.
We **get** to multiply excellence.

When we measure data and statistics, we cannot measure the change we can make within another person's heart. It's not just about the numbers. It's about seeing education as a tool for changing the future of every single one of our students. We must impact their hearts, which will, in turn, impact their minds, which will then impact their future, which eventually changes the world.

The overarching theme of this book is to multiply excellence in those around us, and we do this by continuously enhancing our school's culture. School culture is the hidden curriculum that drives a school forward or backward. A school's culture will do one of two things: empower or defeat a teacher. If teachers feel empowered, this will carry over to the classroom. Unfortunately, if teachers feel defeated, this will carry into classrooms as well.

This book is filled with stories, lessons, and resources that have molded my belief system about what a dynamic school culture is, and what it is not. While much of my career has been spent around elementary aged children, I believe all the ideas, thoughts, and strategies I share about working with both kids and adults can be adapted and used in any school, at any level. A school is only as solid as what it is built on. When relationships are at the root of a school's culture, that is when excellence multiplies. Whether you are a teacher or administrator, my hope is that this book will fill you with a renewed energy, passion, and belief that all kids, regardless of circumstances or socio-economic status, can succeed at high levels.

The book you are about to read is organized into six chapters. Chapter 1 sets the stage for the remainder of the book. In this chapter, you will learn about my personal journey through life, my career pathway, and my core values and beliefs. Chapters 2 through 5 cover Jimmy Casas's four fundamental principles from his book *Culturize* that lay the framework for a positive school culture.

Each chapter will include the following elements:

1. **Systems of Excellence:** Here you will find suggestions for systems you can establish in your classroom or school to create a culture of excellence.

2. **Stories of Success:** Throughout this book, you will come across true success stories about kids, teachers, and parents. Each story begins with a title such as "Michael's Story."

3. **Culture Builders:** At the end of chapters 2 through 5, you will encounter three culture building ideas that you can easily implement in your own classroom or school.

4. **Reflection Questions:** At the end of chapters 2 through 5, you will also find book study questions that will help you to dig deeper into the text, either individually or with colleagues at your school.

When you finish chapter 6, it is my hope that these words have inspired, uplifted, and provided you with the necessary tools to not only live your own excellence, but to multiply excellence in others. May the words in this book fill you with the joyful reminder of why you went into education in the first place—for KIDS.

CHAPTER 1

My Own Journey

I have wonderful memories of a happy childhood in the suburbs of Hoover, Alabama. I grew up in a blended family—my mom's first husband passed away from cancer. Together, they had two kids. My dad, who had never married, was the first single man in the state of Alabama to adopt a son. Time passed, my parents were married, and I was born the very next year. While our family dynamic had its challenges, I was raised in a home with parents who were happily married. As kids, and still today, we have been deeply cared for and loved. My childhood was what many might consider idyllic. More than ever, I am grateful to my parents for the successful pathway they created for me.

When I went into education, I quickly realized that many kids are not afforded the same childhood experiences at home that I had, which results in kids having a more difficult time having natural success in school. Over the last eleven years, I have worked in nine schools with varying demographics and socio-economic status. I've had the experience of teaching 1st, 3rd, and 5th grade, as well as serving as the district math specialist for all of our elementary schools. Currently, I am an administrator at a PreK-5th grade school that houses roughly 600 students. My experiences in varying schools and roles have filled me with a unique perspective about school culture at the elementary level, yet I believe that these experiences are easily adapted to improve classroom and school culture at any grade level. A positive school culture must be firmly rooted in relationships and the belief system that all kids, regardless of **any** circumstance, can reach success.

I began my career as an elementary school educator in a rural district. My last four years in the classroom were spent teaching third grade in a school with a high Hispanic and African American population and over 80% of the students came from low-income families. Our school had a reputation for having the lowest test scores in the district year after year.

If you ever visit the South, you will hear someone use the famous "bless your heart" phrase no less than five times in the span of twenty-four hours. It's our go-to phrase when someone is sick or when someone cracks a joke that wasn't actually funny. Many teachers also love to use this phrase in schools when kids aren't performing as well as we would like. At times, teachers use it as a way to show genuine expression or concern. However, it can also be our way of finding fault in kids without feeling the obligation to do something about it ourselves or believe improvements can be made. When you work at the school with the highest poverty level in the district serving students who are performing at the lowest levels in the district, it can become easy to fall into the trap of adopting the latter mentality if one is not vigilant.

It did not sit well with me that I was working in the lowest-performing school in the district year after year. I was filled with compassion and empathy for my students; however, I was determined to change the perception of our school and change the pathway our kids were on. Why? Simply because our kids deserve better.

The reality was that my students didn't have a desire to be at school. But why? I've always been an upbeat teacher and building positive relationships with kids has always been a strength of mine. So, what was I doing wrong? Let me take you on a journey back to October 2013.

"Ok, boys and girls! It's time for math. Please get out your workbooks and turn to page 126." There were zero smiles, and the students moved like sloths as they pulled their workbooks out of their desks.

"Let's solve number 4. Remember, to find the area, you multiply the length times the width. Who wants to share the answer?"

...Crickets.

"Boys and girls. I am disappointed you aren't paying better attention. What's the answer to number 4?"

A few students raised their hands, maybe 5 out of 24 total. One student had fallen asleep. Another student pulled out a crayon and started coloring his pencil. Was my lesson really so disengaging that a kid decided to color a pencil rather than listen to me? Yep. It was. And you know what? I let the kid keep on coloring. It wasn't his fault that my lesson was boring. It was mine.

I looked around the room as my students compliantly followed suit with the rest of the lesson when it finally hit me. My kids weren't excited about learning. I had created a culture of compliance, at best, and I had to make a change.

It was up to me to determine what I had to do to make my kids want to come back day after day and want to learn. I began developing authentic and engaging lessons that challenged my students' thinking in new and interesting ways.

That same week, the kids had just gotten back from PE when I burst through the door wearing construction worker attire, including a hard hat. You can imagine the look on their faces—eyes wide as saucers, 24 jaws on the floor. I had them EXACTLY where I wanted them!

"Boys and girls. I need your help. I am the lead construction worker for a major housing project in Alabama, and we are looking for the best architects to help us design some new houses. I hear that you all are the best architects in the state of Alabama! Is that true? Now listen, there are some specific guidelines our clients have regarding the area and perimeter of certain rooms in the house. Do you think you can handle this?"

I looked around the room as all 24 of my students looked at me with wonder, shock, and excitement over what was about to happen. I went on to tell them about the lesson and partnered them up. They spent the next few days using their imaginations and creativity to design the perfect dream house for Paschall Construction Company.

Throughout the lesson, there was a beautiful hum of conversations taking place among the students. Every student in the room was talking about the content, and 100% of the students were engaged. The next day my students were begging for more. I had tapped into something that I had not previously done that got them excited about learning and coming to school each day.

By the end of this lesson, I felt joy and passion in my heart. My soul was fueled, and I felt a renewed energy and purpose of why I do what I do each day. I wanted to shout from the rooftops! After experiencing so much success from this lesson, I gradually began building units where the learning was applicable to their world and connections. I held the expectation that ALL kids would reach the same level of success in the end. When we differentiate the expected outcome, that's when we sell kids short. Instead, we must differentiate their journey along the way by scaffolding and frontloading where needed so they are set up to successfully reach their fullest potential. Year after year, my third graders proved their potential with the highest test scores in the district.

My journey as a classroom teacher was a turning point in my career. It taught me that kids—as well as adults—will rise to whatever level of success we *believe* they are capable of. Without this change in my instruction, I would not have become the district math specialist and administrator I am today. We must create classroom and school cultures in which adults and kids fall in love with teaching and learning. Engaging lessons are rooted in authenticity and enthusiasm. If we aren't passionate about what we are teaching, our kids won't be excited to learn. Deliver lessons with passion and joy.

Whatever role you are in, you possess the power to multiply excellence by creating magical learning experiences in your classroom or school every single day. Unleash that power and never look back.

Heart and Mind

As educators, we all have that one person who sparked our passion for education. Mine is Mr. Wade. He was my college professor, and since then he has become a close mentor and friend. Mr. Wade has worn many hats in education, ranging from classroom teacher to Supervisor of Leadership Training in the 7th largest school district in America. Today, at a youthful 74 years of age, he has retired from public education and serves as the principal of a private school in Florida.

With 48 years of educational experience, you can imagine the endless amount of stories Mr. Wade has to tell. His stories about kids leave you feeling empowered and ready to conquer the world of education. During the first session of our Classroom Management class, he had each of us share why we wanted to be a teacher. My confident, yet naive, 20-year-old self said I wanted to become a teacher because I was passionate about improving kids' futures. Sounds like a decent answer, right? Sure, I was zealous and had the best of intentions, but at the time, I thought my passion for teaching curriculum would be the key to reaching kids' hearts. That night, he brought me to tears over a story about one of his former students. It was the first time I had felt emotion about

Whatever role you are in, you possess the power to multiply excellence by creating magical learning experiences in your classroom or school every single day. Unleash that power and never look back.

my future career. In that moment, I realized that education wasn't just a career path I had chosen—it was a calling. Throughout that semester, he taught me that relationships are the gateway to a kid's heart. When we are passionate about reaching kids' hearts, they desire to learn from us, and *then* we can teach them.

Every person we come in contact with has a window of receptivity. Sometimes the window is wide open, or the window may be slightly ajar, with the person waiting to see if they want to open it up fully. We can teach our hearts out, but with the window of receptivity mostly closed, our efforts are futile. If we want to create learners who are intrinsically motivated to succeed, we need to make them feel safe so they will open their window as wide as they can. When that happens, we can go after the heart and create the culture we want. Some teachers are overflowing with academic knowledge, but their passion and care for children isn't there. In order to be an effective teacher and leader, we have to focus not only on the mind, but also on the heart. That is when we create magic in a classroom or school.

When I met Mr. Wade, I felt an instant connection with him. He makes you feel like the most important person in the world when you talk to him. His passion for education pricked my heart on day one, and our friendship has always been very natural. Unfortunately, it isn't always this easy for two people to connect. Regardless of how easy or difficult it is, educators have to be willing to do whatever it takes to connect with kids.

Michael's Story

His name was Michael. Michael was a third-grade student whose home life was in disarray.

Each morning, I stood in the hallways, waiting to greet the kids. "Good morning, Michael!"

Michael looked down toward the floor and hugged the wall until he got past me. This happened every day. Michael rarely smiled at me and avoided interaction with me if at all possible. He exhibited compliant, lackadaisical behaviors during instructional time. My failed attempts at eating lunch with him and playing with him at recess left me feeling frustrated and defeated.

Two months into school. I decided to surprise him by riding his school bus in the morning. We pulled in front of his house and I watched him as he sat by himself on the porch, waiting for the bus to arrive. No one was there waiting with him. His shirt was on inside out, and his hair hadn't been combed. Was I going to be the first person he interacted with today? Michael walked at a snail's pace toward the bus, clearly lacking excitement for his school day to begin.

Michael was the first kid on the bus in the mornings, so this could either create a pivotal moment in our relationship, or it could be a very uncomfortable few minutes until the next student joined us.

"Please, please let this work," I prayed. I desperately needed to reach this kid's heart.

Michael stepped onto the bus and rounded the corner.

"Good morning, Michael!" I said. He looked at me in complete shock and stared at me for a few seconds, which seemed like an eternity. Then he collapsed into my arms for a hug.

"I am so excited to spend some special time with you this morning! I really like your house," I said.

"Thanks! Do you see my bike back there? The red one, not the blue one. That's my brother's. He doesn't know how to ride without training wheels yet, but I do. I can pop a wheelie!"

In that moment, my eyes filled with tears. Finally, after two months, I had made a connection with Michael. He talked my ear off that entire bus ride, and I happily listened to every word, thrilled to the core that his window of receptivity had finally opened up. Now that I had reached his heart, I could unlock a potential in him that he didn't know existed.

You see, anyone can teach from the mind. Don't diminish your effectiveness and power to redirect a child's pathway. When people walk into your school, your *why* should be obvious. Be the premier educator who reaches kids' hearts. When this happens, you will be in the business of transforming lives.

System of Excellence

It is critical that you have a system for everything in your school. If you don't create processes, you have pockets that are not excellent, and that can kill a culture. Throughout this book, you will find suggestions for systems you can establish in your school to ensure you are creating a culture of excellence. We often think about processes regarding safety and discipline. I hope these systems of excellence will help you consider additional processes you can put into practice as you culturize your school. Keep in mind, when you establish new processes in your school, this should be done collectively as one staff, rather than a committee. Committees won't transform a school's culture. In order to reach excellence, all hands must be on deck!

The Dot Project

Every child should feel connected and valued by adults in a school. How are you ensuring that no child slips through the cracks? As a staff, put a system in place to identify these students. Then develop a plan of how you're going to fix the problem. One way a school could do this is by implementing a variation of the Dot Project which I read about in Kim Bearden's book, *Talk to Me*. (Bearden, 2018)

Each year, write every child's name on a sheet of paper. Have your faculty and staff walk around the room placing colored sticker dots on the paper. Have the staff member put their initials on each of their dots.

Red Dot: Place a red dot on the students you have a deep and personal connection with. These are the kids you know everything about—their strengths, weaknesses, hobbies, and aspirations. You feel like you'll keep in touch with this child and their family until the end of time.

Blue Dot: You know a lot about this child and always have a conversation when you see him/her. You have a close connection with this child.

Yellow Dot: You are on a comfort level and have a positive rapport with this child. Maybe this is a former student that you haven't maintained a close bond with.

Tip: If you work in an especially large school, only give each staff member a certain number of dots. Their time and energy are limited.

After you finish, gather the sheets together and categorize them. Have a conversation about what you notice. Which students don't have any dots? These are the kids who are easily forgotten because they aren't connected to staff members in the school.

After every staff member has completed this activity, gather together to discuss these questions:

1. Which students do we need to be intentional about connecting with? How will we make this happen?

2. How can we create opportunities for "yellow dot" or "no dot" students to make connections with one another?
3. How can we find a way to better reach our "yellow dot" or "no dot" families?
4. What are some mentoring programs or clubs we could put into action to enhance opportunities to connect with all kids?

Ideas for how to make your "no dot" students feel more connected:

- Sit with them at lunch.
- Play with them at recess.
- Visit them at home.
- Bring the "no dot" students together at school. Let them share ideas on how you can improve a kid-related matter at school. They will feel much more comfortable to speak up in this setting.

Most importantly, never reveal to a child that he/she is a "no dot" kid. That will make them feel even more isolated. The whole purpose of this is to find a way to make every child in your school feel valued. Be intentional about giving EVERY kid a voice and opportunity to shine.

Unexpected Roadblock

We've all had a curveball thrown at us at some point in our lives. Some-times they sneak up on you when you least expect them. And other times, you know full well that something big is on the horizon. But the truth is, neither option prepares your heart any better for how to react.

Mine came when my husband and I decided we were ready to start growing our family. After four years of trying to have children, we finally decided to reach out to a doctor who could help us get some answers. It was June 2015, and I had just had blood work drawn at the doctor's office when I stopped at a restaurant to have breakfast. While I was there, I got a phone call from my doctor. You know those moments when you just let it keep ringing a few more times, wondering what is about to happen? I remember staring at my phone, knowing that something big was on the horizon. When I picked up the phone, my doctor compassionately told me, "Emily, it's not in the cards. It's not going to happen. You and your husband won't be able to have biological children."

Within seconds, the door was slammed shut for us, and I was instantly broken. I had never experienced this kind of pain, nor did I have any idea of how to handle it. I was grieving the loss of something I had always anticipated for my life. A few days after I found out the news, I remember lying on the couch and telling myself, "Emily it's time to get up. Start moving, even if you don't know where you're going—just move forward." And that's just what I did. I took it one day at a time.

Summer passed by, a new school year began, and I dove into my job as a third-grade teacher. That year, I had a little boy in my class named David. He had white blonde hair, piercing blue eyes, and the sweetest grin that could light up anyone's day. He still has the award of being my favorite student to read a book aloud to. I can still see him tilting his head and grinning with anticipation, wondering what would happen next in the story. When I inflected my voice for different characters, his little mouth would move too. I loved this kid! Sadly, David had his own brokenness in his life. In first grade, his mother was killed in a car wreck. Then in second grade, he went to live with his grandparents, and his grandmother passed away. Now he was in the third grade, in my class, living in a broken, broken world that was totally out of his control.

Before third grade, his academic performance did not line up with his potential. He had never tested on grade level on any assessment, and his grades were average. David and I formed a special relationship that year. He was a brilliant kid, in need of love and consistency, waiting for someone to unveil a world of hope. I was filled with compassion and empathy because of his circumstances; however, I didn't want his circumstances to stunt his potential, and we talked about that often. He ended third grade with the highest scores in our grade level on the state assessment. When we saw the scores the following year, we both cried happy tears.

That year, while I battled my own personal struggles, David's innocence and happiness made an invaluable impression on me. I remember looking at David one day, wishing so badly I could bring him home and help him in the way he needed most, but I knew that was out of my control. And while I couldn't help David in the way that I wanted to, I began to realize there was someone else I could help. Slowly, but surely, my heart was being shaped toward a new calling. A year after finding out our news, my husband and I decided we wanted to adopt a child. Within a week of filling out the paperwork, we were matched with a birthmother, and our beautiful daughter Avery was born 8 months later. While it was a difficult part of my life, I am most grateful to Avery's birth mother for her choice and trust in us to raise Avery. I'm thankful for the journey and for the beautiful lesson I learned along the way: Beauty can come from brokenness if we allow it to. We can become bitter or better; it's up to us.

What is your unexpected roadblock? A diagnosis? A sudden career change? Maybe you have lost someone near and dear to you and you're suddenly living in a world of emptiness and sadness. There are so many ways in which our paths can be redirected, and even though it seems scary in the beginning, we can find that it's actually quite beautiful if we just have faith and LOOK for the beauty. As educators, we have the advantage to use our own experiences to connect with a child. When you are broken, and you are so clouded and can't see the light at the end of the tunnel, look for the opportunity you're not yet seeing. Take time to heal, look for the beauty, and just take it one day at a time.

Kids Do What They Know

"I AM SO TIRED OF TEACHERS IN THIS SCHOOL PICK-ING ON ME. YEAH, I HIT ABBY, BUT I DON'T EVEN CARE. SHE DESERVED IT. GO AHEAD AND PUNISH ME. I COULD CARE LESS. SEND ME TO THE PRINCIPAL'S OFFICE. I DON'T CARE. YOU PEOPLE ARE SO RIDICULOUS."

"Chloe, I will not tolerate you speaking to me like that. That is unacceptable and you know better! I am your teacher and you need to talk to me with respect! Do you understand me?"

Chloe's temper escalated after her teacher responded to her in that way. She actually ended up winning that battle, if we are keeping score. Chloe didn't let anyone have the last word. She was a 5th grade student and had a reputation for making teachers' lives miserable because of her smart mouth and temper. Nobody wanted to have her in their class. We desperately needed to change Chloe's narrative, but how? I called her mom in for a conference to see if we could brainstorm some ways to help Chloe. Here is how the conversation went:

"MRS. PASCHALL, I AM SO TIRED OF PEOPLE PICKING ON MY KID. THIS HAPPENS EVERY YEAR. TELL ME, WHAT DID ABBY DO TO HER TO MAKE HER MAD? SHE PROBA-BLY DESERVED BEING HIT. THIS SCHOOL BETTER STOP SINGLING MY KID OUT OR I'M GOING TO DO SOME-THING ABOUT IT MYSELF. THIS IS RIDICULOUS. I AM SO TIRED OF THIS CRAP."

Minutes later, the mother started screaming at her daughter as they were leaving the school. They ended up in a heated argument that I had to put a stop to, and in that moment, it hit me. Chloe's outbursts were a learned behavior. Chloe *didn't* know better, and shame on me for assuming she did. Perhaps she had never been taught how to have a civilized conversation during conflict. She didn't want to have these outbursts. She simply didn't know how to handle herself any differently. I can't wait for you to read more about Chloe's story later in the book.

When I faced my own personal struggles as an adult, I had no idea how to process or handle them. I'm sure you've been in a situation where you can relate to those feelings. If we don't know how to barrel through our own hardships as adults, how can we expect kids to know how to handle their own adversities, especially when it is the only life they know? So often, we tell kids, "You know better!" but do they? Shaming kids with the "You know better" mentality will lead to compliance, at best, but don't fool yourself into thinking you've fixed the problem. Making a public spectacle of a student's wrong choice is equivalent to bullying—plain and simple. A positive school and classroom culture is rooted with respect, relationships, positive reinforcement, and clear expectations. We aren't in the business of just teaching curriculum. We are in the business of transforming lives and shaping kids' futures.

"When kids can't read, we teach them. When kids can't write, we teach them. So when kids can't behave, why do they get put in the hall?" When I read this quote by Aaron Hogan (Twitter, 2017), it hit me right between the eyes. How many times have I expected a behavior out of a child that they didn't know *how* to exhibit? We can't treat kids at school the same way we treat our kids at home. Why? Because we don't know what is going on in *their* home! During my first year of teaching, I had a student named Jaylen. Jaylen was a bright student, but he had a very difficult time getting along with other kids in the class. When a student upset him or something didn't go his way, his reaction was to hit, pinch, or kick. I was at a complete loss over what I should do to fix this ongoing problem, and I felt like a broken record.

"Jaylen, I am tired of you putting your hands on other students in our class. This isn't the first time you've done this. Today, you hit

Malachi. Yesterday, you hit Joanna. You can't hit someone when something doesn't go your way. I am so disappointed in you. We've talked about this, buddy. You know better."

Jaylen silently looked at the floor. His facial expression showed no remorse, which made me feel more frustrated. I spent the rest of the year battling Jaylen because of his behaviors.

Unfortunately, there is more to the story.

The following school year, Jaylen's dad was arrested for domestic abuse.

I had missed it. My heart ripped to shreds when I read this in the news. While I may not have ever discovered that Jaylen was witnessing abuse in the home, I still missed an opportunity to teach Jaylen a better way to handle his frustrations. We should have high expectations of all kids regarding behavior, but just as we are willing to teach kids about reading and math, we should be equally willing to teach them how to behave in a way that will lead them to success. Teach them, don't shame them! Students deserve for us to communicate and model how we want them to behave. They deserve time to practice new behaviors and chance after chance to improve. Have we ever said "no more chances" to a kid who can't learn how to read? Kids don't make bad decisions just to be bad. There is a root cause behind every behavior. Build a relationship, be their calm, and ask genuine, curious questions to better understand why they are behaving this way. Be at their side as you help them make a change, and extend endless grace and patience, every single time!

System of Excellence

It's important for a staff to have consistency when working with students who don't exhibit appropriate behaviors at school. The more consistent teachers are in how they manage classrooms across grade levels, the better it will be for kids because they will have an easier time adapting from one teacher to the next. As an entire staff, discuss the following questions:

1. What are some appropriate strategies to help a child reflect on and learn from their behavior to prevent history from repeating itself?
2. What are some strategies our school will avoid, such as sending a child to sit in the hall?
3. What strategies and expectations will teachers commit to trying before contacting an administrator?
4. When a child misbehaves, how will you use this as an opportunity to strengthen your relationship with him/her?

This will not only create consistency across your school, but it will also provide teachers the opportunity to learn from one another and reflect on how they can improve their management in the future. Champion kids by helping them reach excellent behavior when they don't know what excellent behavior is.

Home is Where the Start Is

Parents are on the frontline of a child's education. They get to be the first teacher a child experiences, and they are the dominant influence in their lives. Parents play a vital role in creating a student's mindset about school. They either strengthen and reinforce learning, or they can become a barrier to learning, unfortunately. Most parents support their child's education, but what do you do about the parents who seem disinterested? How will you empower them? Many kids go home and listen to their parents talk negatively about school, or worse, about their teacher. What do you do about the parents who don't support you?

I'll never forget the first time I met Mrs. Jones. Mrs. Jones was the mother of Zaria, one of my fifth-grade students. From day one, she made it clear she wasn't thrilled that I was her child's teacher. In my most exciting teacher voice, I introduced myself to Zaria and her mother on the night of Open House. There was an awkward silence that still makes me uncomfortable thinking about it. Zaria looked up at me with a smirk on her face. Her mother looked me in the eye, stared me up and down, and said, "She's going to be a bus rider." Then they went on their way.

Ouch. I had never had that kind of response before when I met a new student, or anyone for that matter. Zaria was new to our school system, and coincidentally, I ran into one of her former teachers that weekend.

"I heard you have one of my former students, Zaria. Good luck! Zaria has a terrible attitude. She's just like her mom. Don't try calling her mom for help. Mrs. Jones will put the blame on you and chew you out. Zaria was one of my lowest-performing students, and she doesn't care anything about school. She won't be disruptive, but don't count on getting her to put forth any effort on her schoolwork. It is going to be a long road with that one."

The first few weeks of school were tough with Zaria. I felt bonded to all my students, except her. One day during reading groups, we were reading a story about the Civil Rights Movement. It was the first time Zaria willingly participated in an academic conversation, and then she said something I'll never forget:

"My mom has told me all about this. She tells me to always make sure I stand up for myself and not let anyone mistreat me. She was bullied in high school because she was black. She still doesn't trust white people today because of it."

When Zaria said that, she made sure to make eye contact with me to be clear that she was sending me the message that she didn't trust me either.

Boom. There it was—I had figured out the root cause behind Mrs. Jones's distrust in me, as well as Zaria's. It wasn't something I had done personally. It was because of something terrible that previously happened to her that left her scarred.

Home is where the start is. I wasn't ever going to build a real relationship with Zaria until I changed her mother's perspective of me.

Zaria loved basketball. That Saturday, I surprised her by showing up to her basketball game. After the game, I had my first conversation with her mom, as well as Zaria's older sister and grandmother. They were shocked to see me there; however, they were cordial. I learned that day that her mom sold Pampered Chef products as a way to make extra money for her family. I asked if she would be willing to send a catalog to school the following Monday.

On Monday morning, Zaria's mother walked into my classroom with the catalog. She still didn't offer any smiles, but she told me about the products she recommended. Baby steps, right? I ordered an egg slicer from her that morning. Then I asked if she would be willing to let Zaria stay after school a few days a week so I could provide her additional help with reading and math.

"How much?" she asked.

"Oh, it's no charge. I just want to help her."

"Seriously? You're going to do this for free?"

"Yes ma'am."

Her mom agreed. For the next few months, I tutored Zaria two days a week after school. After a few weeks of tutoring, Mrs. Jones began hanging out for 5-10 minutes after our tutoring sessions to make small talk. I had finally broken through the barrier with her. Because I had built a relationship with Mrs. Jones, Zaria decided to let me in too. And you know what happened? Zaria ended up being one of the students I grew closest to that year. On the days that I had to give Zaria some tough love because of her lack of effort, her mom backed me up 100%.

You see, it wasn't that Zaria's mom was disinterested in Zaria's education. She had faced her own roadblock that created a barrier from her trusting me as Zaria's teacher. When the barrier was torn down, Mrs.

Jones supported me the rest of the school year. When the school year ended, Zaria was only three months behind grade level in reading, as opposed to 2.5 years behind like she was at the beginning of the year, and she reached grade level proficiency on the math assessment. Zaria, Mrs. Jones, and I celebrated the news by having lunch at Applebee's after we received her scores.

Parental support in a child's education is a major indicator of their academic success. When parents don't accept you at first, don't take it personally. Don't make it about you. Love the kids enough to do whatever it takes to bond with them. Parent-teacher relationships are more than a common courtesy. They are the gateway to creating a positive learning environment for all kids. Oftentimes, to reach the toughest kids, you have to reach the family first. Take time to learn the history so you can help them through it. Home is where the start is! Change their outlook on school. When parents feel valued, then they will value what YOU do. If you want to be an excellent educator, create a community and partnership with parents so that every student is equipped to reach their fullest academic potential.

I can't help but wonder what would have happened if I had allowed Zaria's former teacher to write her story for her. Zaria didn't deserve that. No kid does. Never underestimate the value and importance of relationships. Kids don't learn from people they don't like or trust. Champion kids by taking the time to bond with them, as well as their family. Those are the kids who will come back and thank you for making a difference—for making them feel like somebody when they felt like a nobody. When you end your career, leave behind a legacy of relationships. That is what your kids—and you—will remember.

Culture vs. Morale

How do kids feel about coming to your classroom or school each day? Do they walk into the school each morning with their heads down, avoiding conversation, or do they walk in bright eyed and smiling, ready for the day to begin? Do teachers talk about how they dread coming to work in the mornings, or are they excited for a new day, ready to teach with passion and eagerness? What about the walls inside the school? Are they overflowing with student work, filling the hallways with warmth and color, or are the walls bare, creating a cold, uninviting environment?

If you're working in an environment where kids are excited about coming to school, and staff members love being there each day, you're working in a place where the climate is strong and morale is high; however, that doesn't necessarily mean you have a culture that is firmly rooted with excellence.

Imagine your last data meeting. What kind of responses did you hear? Were the teachers full of excuses for students not achieving?

"This kid didn't have much growth, but remember he is Special Ed. And that kid isn't isn't proficient, but she is ELL, so her reason for scoring so low is because of a language barrier."

Or did the teachers own the data and look at the weaker areas as an opportunity to improve? It's easier to blame poor performance on reasons like poverty and special needs. Many teachers and administrators would rather use these excuses to get us off the hook rather than face the facts, reflect, and ask what we can do better.

What about discipline? Are you constantly putting out fires, such as taking away recess or giving students in-school suspension to teach them that they did something wrong? Or are you taking a restorative approach by giving the child a task that helps them understand what they could have done differently? Situations such as these are where the rubber meets the road with a school's culture.

While culture and morale are both very important to a school, the culture has much deeper roots. Culture has to do with how you're living in the building and what you're doing when no one is watching. Morale is simply a snapshot of feelings at a given time that can unravel in a matter of moments. One cannot get a true picture of a school's culture unless they are a part of it every day.

Don't deceive yourself into thinking your school's culture is strong when morale and climate are high. When we do that, we fall into the dangerous trap of contentment with the status quo and sell kids short of reaching their fullest potential.

> While culture and morale are both very important to a school, the culture has much deeper roots.

The Four Principles of Positive School Culture

Any organization that has encountered long-lasting success is ingrained with an excellent culture. In Jimmy's book, *Culturize*, he covers the four fundamental principles that lay the framework for a positive school culture. The next four chapters of this book are focused on these same four principles, often through the elementary school lens, but applicable to any level. For the remainder of this section, I will provide an overview of each principle as a way to introduce the following chapters. By the end of this book, it is my hope that you will be equipped with what is needed to cultivate and maintain an excellent culture in your classroom, school, and/or school system.

Culturize: To cultivate a community of learners by behaving in a kind, caring, honest, and compassionate manner in order to challenge and inspire each member of the school community to become more than they ever thought possible. (Casas, 2017)

First and foremost, every staff member must understand that a school's purpose for existence is never about the adults in the building. It's always about kids. When we **champion for students,** every decision that is made must be in the best interest of kids. Schools that champion kids hold on

21

to a collective conviction that all kids can reach individual success. Not some. Not most. ALL. Working in education is hard. There are days that leave us feeling discouraged and defeated, but a school that is rooted in a rich culture remains anchored in faith and hope, especially on the toughest days, that every student will achieve at high levels. Championing for kids means envisioning who they can become, rather than dwelling over their shortcomings in the present moment. When educators champion for kids, their desire for every child's success becomes infectious, creating a domino effect that inspires others to follow suit. When you choose positivity by championing kids, so will the rest of your team.

Secondly, it should be understood that all staff members **expect excellence** of one another, and, most importantly, of the kids they serve. Being average or even "good enough" is actually not good enough. Don't settle for that. Average expectations maintain a child's current reality, or worse, cause regression. Adults and kids will rise to whatever expectations we have of them. We should have the highest expectations for kids regarding both academics and behavior. When we blame non-achievement on socio-economic status or "ability" according to standardized test scores, we are saying that certain kids can't achieve excellence. Don't go there. Always expect excellence. Every child has an untapped potential that can be unlocked with the right relationships and instruction. Set the bar high for others and yourself and mean it when you say you believe in your students. Belief in one's own ability to achieve excellence is the best gift we can give a child.

The third core principle is that you always **carry the banner** for your school. The strength of a school, just like a family, is contingent on its loyalty to each other. Students, teachers, parents, and community members are equally responsible for communicating a positive perception of your school at all times. Carrying the banner does not equate to circulating information. It means showcasing the great things that are happening for kids in your school every day so that there is no room left for assumptions. Tell your school's story, or someone else will. The people who work inside a school set the tone more than anyone else. Love your school every day and let the joy of teaching be written all over your face. Going to school and getting to be around kids isn't merely a job; it's a calling. Your attitude is contagious, and when it is positive and encouraging, others will follow.

> Championing for kids means envisioning who they can become, rather than dwelling over their shortcomings in the present moment.
>
> ∼

When you carry the banner for your school, it opens doors to build positive relationships, not just with coworkers in your school, but across the entire community. Why? Because we are all invested in the same purpose of working toward the greater good—changing lives and shaping kids' futures. Your school's banner should be so infectious that other people in the community are carrying it for you. Showcase your school in a way that makes everyone want to be a part of it.

Finally, every staff member in the building must aspire to **be a merchant of hope** to kids. Many kids are living in a world of despair and can't see a way out. While we don't have control over their circumstances, we have the power to build relationships, ignite imaginations, and inspire hope. Give them a purpose to keep moving forward. Teaching is not only a job, but a service. We can't change the past; however, don't underestimate the power you have to change a child's present and future. Our students' potentials are limitless. Have faith. Show tenacity, offer endless grace, and plant seeds of hope one child at a time.

A strong school culture doesn't happen by fluke. It stems from a staff who strategically and intentionally works toward accomplishing a common vision. This book is not filled with the magical recipe on how to fix all of the problems in education. Rather, it is filled with stories and ideas about how to lay a foundation of core principles for your school to rely on so that you can develop a common language, belief system, and expectations—and thus multiply excellence—within your school.

Don't let yourself fall into the trap of contentment with the status-quo. Mediocrity should never be the standard. You are so much better than that, and kids deserve better. Our profession contributes more to the future of our world than any other profession on earth. You hold the capacity to have a drastic influence and impact on kids' lives. Reawaken your passion, remember your why, and believe in your ability to be awesome at what you do. Jump in headfirst, and don't look back!

CHAPTER 2

Core Principle 1: Champion for Students

Championing kids must begin with the simple yet crucial understanding of a school's purpose for existence. Adam Welcome and Todd Nesloney nailed it when they made this statement: "Schools don't exist so adults can have jobs. Schools exist for students. And our job is about making kids feel confident by embracing them for who they are." (Nesloney & Welcome, 2016, p. 135).

It's not about us. It's about kids, and when we come into contact with the students in our school, they should be left feeling like the most important people in the world.

Take it to the House

"The ability to be in the present moment
is a major component of mental wellness."

Abraham Maslow (Maslow, n.d.)

Take a moment to let those words sink in. Who are the kids in your school that are struggling to function because they are weighed down with stressors from home that no child should ever have to worry about? More importantly, what are you doing about this? Maslow's Hierarchy of Needs states that when kids are deprived of their physiological and psychological needs, they lack the motivation to become the best version of themselves. (Maslow, 2018) What steps are you taking to fulfill your students' needs so that all kids have equitable access to reach their full potential? In order to champion kids, we must be tuned in to all five tiers of this model to know where our students' deficiencies lie.

Stephen's Story

"Hi Stephen, how are you today?"

Crickets.

"Good morning Stephen! Did you have a good weekend?"

Crickets.

"Hey Stephen, could I get you to help me with something?"

Crickets.

Stephen was a fourth-grade student who was selectively mute when he was not in the safety of his own home. Time and time again, I tried to connect with Stephen, and time and time again, I hit a brick wall. Stephen had faced a great deal of childhood trauma in his short lifetime. His parents neglected him, and he lived with his grandmother, who was his safety blanket. They had no access to transportation, struggled to get food on the table, and didn't make enough money to make ends meet. According to Maslow's Hierarchy of Needs Model, Stephen had a deficiency in all five tiers.

Mid-year, Stephen suddenly began showing defiant, erratic behaviors at school, including refusal to comply with directions, disrupting class, and intentionally attempting to harm himself. He was crying for help in the only way he knew how, but with his mutism, I was having zero success reaching him.

One Saturday, our Director of Federal Programs, Allison Usery, and I contacted the grandmother requesting to conduct a home visit. On our way there, I emotionally told Allison, "I don't even know what this kid's voice sounds like. How can I help a child whose window of receptivity is sealed shut? This home visit has to be our breakthrough to reaching Stephen. It has to." When we arrived, we sat on the couch and talked with his grandmother about the resources we could offer her to lighten her burden of living in poverty. Stephen sat on the couch a few feet away from me, slowly inching closer and closer with the shyest and sweetest grin on his face.

"Do you wanna hear me play my guitar, Mrs. Paschall?"

Those were the first words I ever heard Stephen say. Ten words that will stick with me for the rest of my life. Ten words that made me grin from ear to ear. Stephen had the sweetest, most innocent voice. I'll never forget the burst of happiness that shot through me in that moment. I sat there and listened to him play his guitar for a few minutes, and then he invited me to his room where we played video games and chatted about his favorite things.

In the comfort of Stephen's home, Allison and I were able to meet his physiological and safety needs. In the comfort of Stephen's home, I heard his voice for the first time. In the comfort of Stephen's home, we championed Stephen and his grandmother.

Were all of Stephen's problems solved after this day? Of course not. But for the first time, we were moving in the right direction. I can confidently say I would never have made a connection with Stephen had I not taken it to the house. Stephen had extreme anxiety and trust issues, and he needed to be in his safe place before he would willingly let me connect with him.

Visiting a child's home:

- illuminates a child's current reality to a teacher. When you understand their environment, you're better equipped to meet their needs in the classroom.
- increases the chances that a parent will be in their comfort zone. Phone calls and parent conferences at school can seem impersonal. When you travel to their home, they are more likely to open their window of receptivity.
- creates a partnership. So often, we find ourselves calling home for a negative reason such as struggling grades or behavior. Home visits provide an opportunity for collaboration.
- helps a child to see they have a network of support. So many kids feel like they are on an island with no support at home. Create that support system for them by bridging the school to home connection.
- increases the chance that a parent will become more involved. When parents feel connected to their child's teacher, chances increase that they will be motivated to be involved in their child's learning experience.

Home visits are a valuable—and vastly underused—way to connect with a child and their family. I believe that educators love kids, but if we want to be in the business of championing kids, we've got to love the family as well. Don't say you've tried everything until you've tried to reach the child and family in the comfort of their own home. Don't let fear get in the way. Sometimes, it is the only way to reach a child. When we partner with and empower parents, we multiply the chance that all kids will reach their personal excellence. Reach new heights in your level of impact by taking it to the house!

System of Excellence

Over the years, I've come across many teachers and administrators who are hesitant to go on a home visit, for various reasons:

- It's out of my element.
- I wouldn't feel comfortable.
- It's risky.
- I don't see the value.
- I wouldn't be comfortable with people coming into my house.
- I don't have the time.

Can you relate to one of these reasons?

If you have never conducted home visits in your schools, brainstorm how you can begin doing them in a way that feels comfortable for you and your colleagues. My advice would be to begin doing these for a positive reason. Home visits don't always have to be negative or reactionary.

Before school starts, create a process where staff members visit every child's home. Let the parents know ahead of time that you'll be coming so they are prepared.

Here are some ideas on how you can begin home visits with a positive approach:

- Deliver a yard sign to every child and take their picture for the upcoming school year.
- Do you work in a school with a large percentage of students who come from poverty? Use your Title I funds to deliver school supplies to every child.
- Bring the kids a snack.

Once you have gotten your feet wet with this, it will be much easier to go on home visits when it subsequently becomes necessary to visit for a less pleasant reason such as attendance, behavior, or physiological needs. When you approach a family with sincerity and compassion, chances are high they will receive your care with open arms.

Don't let fear get in the way of you going on home visits. If you do, this could become the barrier that keeps your school from reaching excellence.

Compliance vs. Intrinsic Motivation

I once overheard this conversation between two teachers:

Teacher A: "I'm just a black and white person. I don't do well with the kids who don't want to do their schoolwork. I'm not so sure Kayla is going to make it in my class this year."

Teacher B: "Why doesn't she want to do her schoolwork?"

Teacher A: "She doesn't like me, so she just doesn't try in my class."

Teacher B: "Why doesn't she like you?"

Teacher A: "Because I am a stickler, and I am going to make her behave."

Teacher B: "Well, is your approach working?"

Teacher A: "No. I guess not. Plus, she always tells me my lessons are boring."

Teacher B: "Well, are they?"

Teacher A: "I don't know. She apparently thinks so! What did you do last year to get her to engage? I'm desperate."

Teacher B: "I focused on making connections and building relationships, not compliance. And then I found out what got them excited about learning."

Compliance. It's one of those words that makes me cringe when a teacher thinks it is the key to getting kids to learn. But is compliance always a bad thing? No. In some ways, it is necessary. When the tornado drill sounds, kids should comply and take necessary actions toward safety. But compliance should never be our end goal in the classroom.

Take a look at the true definition of the word:

Compliant: inclined to agree with others or obey rules, especially to an excessive degree.

Is this what we want for our students? Do we want kids who simply

> Compliance. It's one of those words that makes me cringe when a teacher thinks it is the key to getting kids to learn. But is compliance always a bad thing? No. In some ways, it is necessary. When the tornado drill sounds, kids should comply and take necessary actions toward safety. But compliance should never be our end goal in the classroom.
>
> ～

31

obey rules and do as they are told? Or do we want students who are excited about their future and intrinsically motivated to learn more?

We get to work in a profession that prepares kids for all future professions. Why wouldn't we teach in a way that gets kids excited about that, even at five years old? Kids tend to do what they enjoy doing. Can we blame them? Instead of putting kids in a box and expecting them to learn in a way that makes lesson planning easier for us, teachers should be stepping outside of the box and planning lessons that result in students begging for more.

Christian's Story

Christian was one of those kids who could easily get lost in a crowd. He was the student who let the other kids answer the questions during a lesson so that he could get away with slipping through the cracks. Christian had a history of chronic absenteeism and missed 40+ days of school each year. He repeated the first grade because he was so behind due to his absences. Christian was a well-mannered kid, never disruptive during instructional time; however, he didn't care about learning. He was simply compliant on the days he was at school.

It was the second week of school, and I was having a difficult time getting Christian excited about being there. Each day, I excitedly greeted him in the hallway and always received a solemn, "Hey" in return. He would mosey his way into my classroom and go straight to his desk. Christian hadn't missed a day of school yet, but I knew in my gut the day was coming.

One day at recess, I brought my tennis shoes outside (which was not uncommon) and asked who wanted to play kickball. The entire class screamed with excitement, and I picked Christian to be the captain. Athleticism was not one of Christian's strengths, so he was a bit shocked; however, he happily accepted the role. I then watched Christian ask all the students to line up so he could more easily select the teams. He went on to explain the rules of the game, and he did it with such clarity. He had the full attention of every kid in the class.

"What just happened?" I thought. This kid was a leader! Who knew I would discover this talent of his during a game of kickball?

"Christian, I was really impressed with how you handled our class today. You had so much confidence, and you explained the rules of the games so clearly. Could I count on you to help out with more things like that in the future?"

"Yeah, I guess so."

Now, that may seem like an indifferent response. Sure, he played it cool in the moment, but then he walked away to go and tell the first person he saw what I had just said to him.

As the school year went on, I learned that Christian was a brilliant mathematician—one of the strongest math students I ever had in my years of teaching. He could do mental math better than I could. There were many days that Christian would lead our 10 minute "Mental Math" lesson. He was a great teacher, and I couldn't help but smile every time I watched him lead the lessons. He was completely different from the kid I met on the first day of school. Because I tapped into his strengths, his self-esteem grew, and he was excited about learning. He didn't want to miss out on anything!

Christian missed less than ten days of school that year. And on the days he was absent, you better believe I called home every single time to let him know how much we missed him. He always assured me he would be back the next day, ready to lead.

"Lifelong learner" is one of the buzzwords we often throw around in education. Lifelong learners desire to learn. They aren't compliant. When we use that phrase, let's be sure we truly understand what we are saying.

Kids need constant cheerleaders in their lives to tell them when they are doing something great, to guide them when they need redirecting, and to be behind the scenes setting up the perfect storm for them to discover their strengths. If we want to champion all students, we need to help them find their place where they feel connected, appreciated, and loved.

System of Excellence

The meaning of life is to find your gift.
The purpose of life is to give it away.

Pablo Picasso.

We typically do a great job of untapping talents from our natural born leaders, but what about the rest of the students? What can you do to enhance leadership opportunities for all kids in your school? I'm not asking you to create an extravagant plan where every child is given a major leadership role. That's not best for every kid; however:

Every child should feel valued.
Every child needs a purpose.
Every child has a gift.

Take a few minutes to write every students' name down on a piece of paper. Beside their names, write down their God-given, unique trait that will carry them far in life. If you haven't discovered it, ask their previous teachers. If they don't know, this is likely a student who is slipping through the cracks.

Below are some ways you can build leadership capacity in all kids:

- Peer Helpers - Students who have—or wish to strengthen their—strong soft skills can apply to become a peer helper. Peer helpers can be morning greeters, take new students on school tours, and greet visitors on days when there are special events. Peer helpers can also mentor other students who need support in coping with their emotional or behavioral skills.

- Peer Tutor - Students who have a strength in academics can become a tutor to students who need more support.
- News Anchor - Students who enjoy public speaking would benefit from becoming a morning news anchor. Create opportunities for them to utilize their strengths.
- Media Team - Allow students proficient in tech skills to serve on your media team. They can record and edit the daily news for the school.
- Social Media Team -Allow your students who have an interest in photography and social media to make "kid posts" on your social media sites. What better way is there to teach kids about Digital Citizenship?
- Art/Music Helpers - Do you have students who have strong artistic skills? Allow them to apply to be an assistant to the art and music teachers in your school.

The ideas are endless. The important thing is that you create opportunities for every child to feel that their unique abilities are valued.

Administrators, while it isn't feasible for you to write down every students' name, you can still model this community building activity in a staff meeting. Supply every staff member with a piece of paper that states their unique trait. Better yet, read or project it for everyone to see. Kids are not the only ones who need recognition for their strengths. Additionally, it is important that you, the school leader, recognize others' strengths so you can intentionally utilize them to culturize your school.

When we are intentional about giving kids a purpose for coming to school beyond just being there to learn, you will be shocked at the change in their outlook on school. Every kid has a unique talent. They are just waiting for us to untap it.

Drop Back and Punt

Achievement Gap.

It is another commonly used buzzword in education that describes the kids who start off behind, even before school begins. The term "achievement gap" refers to the discrepancy in academic outcomes between lower-income or minority students and their affluent peers. Where the danger lies is when we begin to believe that the conditions and roadblocks kids are born into determine their opportunities in life.

> Achievement gaps don't exist because of a child's innate ability. They exist because educators haven't discovered the students' true interference.

Achievement gaps don't exist because of a child's innate ability. They exist because educators haven't discovered the students' true interference.

Maybe the interference stems from inequities in the home, such as internet access.

Maybe the interference is due to a language barrier.

Maybe the interference exists because a child lacks real world experiences.

As educators, it is our job to figure out what the learning interference is so that we can remove the barrier and lead every child toward academic success.

When I taught third grade, over 80% of my students were identified as living in economically disadvantaged households. The majority of my students were Hispanic or African American, and many of them struggled academically due to a language barrier or specific learning disability. Our kids were the lowest-performing students in the district, so naturally there were many days that I had to drop back and punt and reteach in a different way the following day. We've all had those days where our perfectly planned lessons completely flopped, where the kids just didn't get it. What did you do about it? Did you blame it on a child's situation, such as a language barrier, disability, or home life? Or did you self-reflect and find a way to reach them? What sets an excellent teacher apart from others is how s/he handles these failed attempts. Failure is not the end result, rather it is a stepping stone toward success. It's an opportunity to grow by trying again and making improvements.

It was the middle of my first year of teaching third grade. I had taught the author's point of view the previous week until I was blue in the face, but the majority of my class still failed the assessment.

"What HAPPENED?" I thought.

When I reflected on my previous lessons, their interference hit me like a ton of bricks. You see, the majority of the text our reading curriculum provided to teach the author's point of view was about white women who stood up for inequality in America. While these were great stories about women who made a difference, the reality was that I only had two white girls in my class. The majority of my students couldn't relate to these women; therefore, they didn't connect with the text to master the skill. It wasn't that my students were inadequate. They weren't connected, which resulted in disengagement.

The following week, we learned about point of view, but this time I included text about African and Hispanic American men and women who have made an impact on our world. The students had the opportunity to choose the text we read in their reading group. They loved it. Not only did they master the skill relating to the author's point of view, but they also wrote papers stating whether they held the same opinion as the author. What I had anticipated taking nearly a month to teach ended up only taking a week and a half. In the following weeks, we were able to go much deeper with the learning through debates, presentations, and opinion writing. My students blew me away with their capabilities! When we incorporate what matters to our students into our lessons, they will re-engage and express a desire to learn.

You see, it wasn't an achievement gap that existed among my students. It was an instructional gap. All this time, I had been holding them back from their fullest potential because I had not considered what was important to them.

Kids need to see themselves through our teaching. If we don't allow this to happen, we're simply saying they don't matter.

When our students don't learn, it isn't because they lack the necessary life experiences to succeed. It is because we haven't yet tapped into the true learning barrier. Integrate your students into your teaching so they see themselves in the lessons and have a purpose for learning. That is when you will create magic in the classroom.

When I was an instructional coach, I modeled a lesson centered around a fairly difficult word problem in a first-grade classroom:

Daniel bought 17 pumpkins at the farm. 8 of the pumpkins were white. The rest were orange. How many orange pumpkins did he buy?

The lesson was hands-on, engaging, and full of pictures and discussion. At the end of the lesson, all but one student mastered the skill. The remaining student was a Hispanic girl.

Her teacher whispered to me, "Oh Mrs. Paschall, she has to come back for intervention every day. She just struggles in math. I am at a loss. I don't know how to help her."

I pulled her to the small group table, hoping I could find the interference.

She was able to explain the story problem to me, but she couldn't figure out what she needed to do with the Unifix cubes she was using to represent her pumpkins.

After a few minutes of failed questioning, I finally asked this simple question:

"Amelia, do you know what "the rest" means?

"No ma'am."

"It means the amount that is leftover. Can you point to the amount that is leftover?"

"Oh! So, it's the pumpkins that aren't white?"

"Yes!"

Immediately, Amelia pulled nine of the counters to the side to represent the amount that were orange. She automatically knew the answer without having to count them. Wow! Amelia was bright! The next day, she completed this task without hesitation.

Once again, it wasn't an achievement gap that kept Amelia from reaching success. It was an instructional gap. The term achievement gap is a cop out that prevents us from helping kids reach success. Never let a child's interference excuse them from achieving at the same level as the rest of their peers. The interference isn't due to their circumstances. The interference is in the instruction. I prefer the term "instructional gap" because it places the focus back on us as teachers to self-reflect and make an instructional adjustment. Don't lower your standards when kids don't succeed the first time.

Never allow a child's label to hold them hostage from learning. Champion for kids by changing your methods to reach them and bring them where they need to be. Scaffold, scaffold, scaffold. All kids can succeed. Sometimes you just have to adjust the journey along the way. Where we mess up is when we change the expected outcome. Schools with a healthy culture never lower the expectations they have for their students' performance. At times, we must simply drop back and punt, but keep the bar high and always try again.

System of Excellence

Every day, there will be students who do not initially meet the learning target. It's inevitable. We can't always predict what a child's interference will be. Sometimes it's your students who consistently need additional support, while other times it may be a non-struggling student who had an isolated interference that day.

Regardless of who it is, every single student deserves infinite chances to reach their full potential. Do you have a structure in place to ensure that teachers bridge instructional gaps each day?

Create an expectation where teachers have an allotted time in their daily schedule to "drop back and punt" for the kids who need a second opportunity to work toward mastery of the standards they are learning that week. This intervention time should be dedicated toward grade level standards, separate from the intervention time we devote to the students who are below grade level.

Below are some reflective questions teachers should ask themselves daily:

- What are the anticipated learning interferences my students may face that I need to proactively prepare for?
- What is my learning target?
- How will I know when the students have met the learning target?
- What was the interference in my instruction?
- How will I approach this skill in a different way during intervention to help the child reach success?

With this system of excellence in place, you'll provide all kids an equitable opportunity to reach their full potential. Without it, instructional gaps will pile on top of one another until it reaches a point where it would be very hard for a child to catch up.

Be relentless, promote equity, and call the learning interference what it truly is: an instructional gap. When you shift this mentality, you will be well on your way to championing all kids as they work toward academic success.

Sometimes It's Best to Shut Up and Listen

Alex's Story

"Mrs. Paschall, I have Alex here with me, and I am so disappointed in her today. She has been snippy with other kids in the class, and she has had an attitude toward me all morning. I can't get her to complete any of her work. I have given her chance after chance today, but she has made no change in her behavior."

Alex's eyes filled with tears. She put her head down in shame and remained completely silent. Mrs. Edgemont left my office so that Alex and I could have a minute to chat alone.

"Alex, I can tell you're very upset right now. Can you help me understand what is upsetting you?"

She remained silent. I could tell she needed a minute to get control of her emotions.

"Would it help if you looked at some of my picture books for a few minutes to help you calm down a bit?"

"Yes ma'am."

"Go for it. Let me know when you'd like to talk. And just know this: I care about you, Alex. I'm not mad at you. I just want to help. Think about that while you look at the books, ok?"

Ten minutes passed by, and Alex let me know she was ready to talk.

"My dad went to jail last night."

Immediately, Alex melted into a puddle of tears. She went on to explain that he had been involved in a hit and run, as well as illegal drug use, that resulted in him going to jail. Alex had only had one hour of sleep, she didn't have dinner the night before, and she was too upset to eat breakfast or lunch the next day.

Exhaustion. Worry. Hunger. Frustration.

Alex was being faced with all of these emotions at once. Of course she wasn't in a state where she could complete her work. After talking about her situation for several minutes, I ended the conversation with this last statement:

"Alex, tell me what you need right now to help you feel better so that you can have a good rest of the day at school."

"Can I lie down? And have something to eat?"

"Absolutely."

I took her to the cafeteria to get her something to eat. Then she went to the nurse's office to rest her eyes for the next hour. When she woke up, she felt much better and was ready to go back to class.

Sometimes, we just need to shut up and listen. We have no idea what kids face during the hours they are not at school.

When I told her teacher what had happened, she buried her hands in her face, disappointed in herself for not figuring this out on her own. Hey, we've all been there. I know I have. It is difficult for teachers to force themselves to slow down and discover the "why" behind a child's behaviors. Becoming an administrator has illuminated all of my missed opportunities to better understand a kid when I was a classroom teacher. It's amazing what we can learn about kids when we take the time to ask the right questions, rather than shaming them for their choices.

Seek first to understand. This is hard for adults. We instinctively want to tell kids what they should have done differently without ever trying to understand the root cause of their actions. Kids don't make bad decisions just for the sake of being bad. Ask questions that will help you understand the cause of their actions. Adults haven't been a kid in a long time. We shouldn't expect kids to respond to situations like we would as an adult. Remember they have been in this world for a decade or less. Put yourself in their shoes. Look through the lens of a child by trying to understand their perspective and point-of-view.

Listen. Genuinely listen to kids. Sit beside them, not across. If you can't sit, squat down to their level. When we stand over a child, we make them feel embarrassed and humiliated. Do everything in your power to make them feel comfortable so they will feel safe to be open and honest with you.

Ask questions. Allow kids time to discover how they could have handled the situation differently. Ask questions that will lead the child to develop a positive solution. Guide them, don't shame them.

When you demonstrate that you're simply wanting to have a conversation, you will be able to guide the conversation toward a meaningful resolution. Model the behavior you want to see in others. To champion kids, we must love them enough to do this.

Teachers love to be in control. It is a huge part of what makes us so great at what we do, but in order to champion kids, we've got to know when to relinquish it and put the control back in the child's hands.

One year, I had an especially rambunctious fifth grade class. I always taught reading first thing in the morning with our math lesson immediately following. Every single day, without fail, I struggled to keep three of my highest achieving students on task. I went above and beyond to ensure the lessons were engaging, exciting, hands-on—you name it! No matter what I tried, these three students still struggled to engage themselves in the lesson, and as a result, their grades were suffering. Finally, after exhausting all my efforts, I asked them how I could help them stay on task. I'll never forget what Jaylen said to me:

"Mrs. Paschall, my brain needs a break! I am too tired to start math right after we finish reading each day."

The others chimed in and agreed. They were exhausted after two hours of reading. Two of these three students had been diagnosed with Attention Deficit Hyperactivity Disorder. Of course they needed a break.

The next day, we had a ten-minute brain break between our reading and math lesson where the kids had the freedom to choose how they used their time to let their brains rest. It didn't just improve the three students' attention spans; it positively impacted the entire class. As a result, we had a brain break every day for the rest of the school year.

If I had not had a conversation with those three students, I wouldn't have known what their interference was.

Sometimes it's best to simply "shut up and listen." Kids are experts at being kids. Many times, they know exactly what their interference is, as well as what they need in order to improve. Champion kids by asking them how you can help and be ready and willing to adjust and make a change.

Tackle the Barriers to Student Success

Giving up on kids is never the answer. Teachers must be relentless and willing to do whatever it takes to tackle a student's barriers to success. For some kids, that may mean providing extra time to complete their work so they can rise above their disability. For others, it means bending over backwards. While both instances are equally important, one will certainly take more of an emotional toll on us than the other.

Isaiah's Story

Isaiah joined my third-grade class in October, after being told he could no longer attend his former school because he was living out of district. Isaiah was one of those students you immediately recognized as a 9-1-1 emergency. He had failing grades and weighed over 200 pounds. He still wore diapers, and his hygiene was an issue because of his toileting problems. You can imagine that he had a hard time making friends. He had a page full of discipline write-ups from his previous school, zero desire to learn, and was chronically absent. To put the cherry on top, his family was completely dysfunctional. Isaiah was a total cry for help.

On his first day of school, I walked down to the front office to meet Isaiah and his mother before they came to my class.

"Hi Isaiah! My name is Mrs. Paschall! I am so excited to meet you. The other boys and girls are thrilled to be getting a new student. And you must be Isaiah's mom, Ms. Blankenship, correct? I am so excited to have your son joining our class."

His mom stared at me for a second, looked at Isaiah, and looked back at me.

"Good luck with this one. He is awful and won't listen to anything you say. I left extra diapers and clothes with the nurse. Call me if you need me."

After the mom said these things, I glanced over to see Isaiah's reaction. He was looking at the decorations on the wall, seemingly unphased. It was an instant clue that these types of comments were a normalcy for him. He didn't know any different. I had never heard a parent speak about their child in this way, especially right in front of them. I was dumbfounded.

"Well I cannot wait to get to know both of you and learn together what makes him special. I'll be in touch!"

Weeks passed, and Isaiah had completely changed our classroom dynamic. I'm going to be very candid with you: I was struggling. Isaiah's defiant behaviors stressed the other students (and me) out. He didn't get along well with others, and the kids were turned off by his lack of personal hygiene. He was disruptive during instructional time, and he showed zero desire to want to improve. No matter what I tried, I couldn't seem to build a positive relationship with him. I'm sure you've been there. We've all had "that one kid," right?

After exhausting all my own attempts, I gathered troops of behavior specialists from our central office to help. We had a meeting with his mother to create a behavior plan which included social, academic, and toileting goals. In that meeting, we listened to his mother talk about how ashamed she was of him. She had given up on him long ago, and she admitted that her life would be so much easier if he lived with his dad. Isaiah had no one championing for him in his life—no one—and it completely broke my heart.

As time passed, we were seeing small successes with his behavior plan in place, but in my gut, I knew there was still a superficial relationship between Isaiah and me. In the few moments he showed positive behaviors, his motivation was extrinsic, never intrinsic. How would I inspire Isaiah to have the inner desire to improve his quality of life?

It was the last day of school before Christmas break, and Isaiah was absent, which was not uncommon, but sadly, he missed our Christmas party. When school let out, I marched down to my principal's office, with my keys in one hand and Isaiah's Christmas presents in the other.

"Where are you headed?" my principal asked.

"I'm going to Isaiah's house for a home visit. When his mom answers the door, I am going to use the excuse that I wanted to give Isaiah his Christmas presents. I desperately need to reach this kid's heart, and I have exhausted all other ideas on how to make this happen within the four walls of my classroom. So, I'm praying it will happen in his own home."

My principal smiled, grabbed her purse, and said, "I'm coming with you."

We knocked on the door, and his mother answered.

"What do y'all want?" she asked in a gruff, uninviting voice.

"Hey! I missed Isaiah at school today. I wanted to give him his Christmas presents before the break."

She stared at us in complete shock. Then she hesitantly opened the door to let us in.

"Mrs. Paschall? What are you doing here?" Isaiah asked.

"Hey buddy! I came to see you! I was so sad you missed our Christmas Party. I didn't want to wait three weeks to give your gifts to you!"

For the first time, Isaiah smiled at me—truly smiled—and he gave me the biggest bear hug. It was one of those moments we live for as teachers, one that I will never forget. I was finally tackling the barrier to his success - he desperately needed a champion, and he was starting to trust that I longed to be that person for him.

We stayed for about an hour. For the first fifteen minutes, his mom was in defense mode, ranting about how much she disliked our school and how difficult life was at home because of Isaiah. After listening for some time, I diverted the conversation and began telling her the positive things that had happened with Isaiah at school and how proud I was of him. Her anger shifted to tears of sadness as she began sharing her personal life struggles with us. You see, she wasn't angry at our school or at Isaiah for that matter. She was broken because of her own choices, and she was looking for anyone to blame but herself. You couldn't help but feel sorry for her.

For the rest of our visit, Isaiah and his younger brother showed us their bedrooms and some of their favorite toys. Before we left, I told Isaiah how much I loved him. This wasn't the first time Isaiah had heard me say that, but in that moment, I knew he believed me, and for the first time, he responded back with, "I love you, too." Before we left, I hugged his mom and told her how much I cared about her son. With tears in her eyes, she thanked me and wished us, "Merry Christmas."

Everything with Isaiah was different after that day. Did he become the model student? No, but I never expected that. For the first time in his life, he desired to make positive changes, not just for me, but for himself. And he did.

Home is where the start is. Never underestimate the power of visiting a child's family in their own home. Chances are you will not only open the child's window of receptivity, but also the family's.

Giving up on kids is never the answer. Ever. Whatever the barrier may be, teachers must reach out with endless love and compassion. Champion for kids by tackling their barriers to success. Let them know you are ready to carry them through the waves of any storm they may face—ANY STORM—and follow through by offering your hand every single time.

Leaders Create a Plot Twist

"Relationships, relationships, relationships +
Time Invested = Culture"

Jimmy Casas (Casas, 2019)

If you want to know about the culture of a school, listen to the conversations that take place in a data meeting. Observe how the teachers and administrators talk about the students who struggle academically and/or behaviorally. You will hear one of two things: Either teachers have a relentless, whatever-it-takes mentality to lead all kids toward success, or they are reeking with excuses designed to tactfully "write off" academically and behaviorally challenging kids from reaching their full potential.

"Shaun's data hasn't moved because he just doesn't want to put forth any effort. He's not motivated, and I don't know how you fix that."

Excuse.

"My low kids didn't make as much progress, but I wouldn't expect them to grow as much as the rest of the class anyway."

Excuse.

"Joanna didn't make any progress, but bless her heart, she's a special education student."

Excuse.

"When we give up on a student out of frustration, anger, or
because their behavior or performance convinces us they don't
care, we give up our power to influence them in a positive way.
When we don't believe they can, rest assured they won't."

Jimmy Casas (Casas, 2019)

Teaching is a hard job, arguably one of the toughest jobs in the world. Trying to teach students who are three years behind grade level, have challenging behaviors, or lack motivation makes the job difficult, to say the least. We feel like we don't have enough time to plan, and at times, it seems like all of the plates we are asked to spin each day is completely impossible. We feel frustrated when we lose freedom to make decisions in our classroom as a result of state expectations. All these factors make it easy to feel like we have been set up for defeat. I get it. I've been there. Regardless of whatever hardships we face as teachers, we cannot fall prey to allowing these difficulties to become an excuse for not giving our everything toward the mission of education: helping every child reach success.

The moment a child starts attending school, they unknowingly begin to write their school narrative that they will carry with them the rest of their life. Some narratives are seamless, filled with stories about a wonderfully behaved child who got along well with others and loved learning. Other kids' stories may have hiccups along the way, with choices made here and there that taught them tough lessons about character and perseverance. Then there are the kids whose school narratives are a complete train wreck. Regardless of the story they have begun to write for themselves, as teachers we must believe in our power to change the narrative for those who need it the most. The best books in life have a major turning point. Champion kids by creating their narrative plot twist toward success!

Jeremy's Story

It was my first month of being an assistant principal in a new school.

"Mrs. Paschall, you are needed in the office. Jeremy and his teacher are headed down to see you. "

Jeremy.

Everyone in the school knew who Jeremy was—EVERYONE. It wasn't easy for Jeremy to make choices that set him up for successful days at school. When I arrived at my office, Jeremy was slumped down in one of my chairs with his hood over his head. He was in a rage, yelling at anyone who came in contact with him.

I watched his teacher handle him with complete patience and compassion. She sat with him to help him as he worked through his emotions. As he slowly began to de-escalate, she gave him the gift of time by allowing him a few moments to decompress. When he was ready, they discussed what triggered his outburst, his feelings toward the situation, and how he could have responded differently.

Later that morning, his teacher came to talk to me about Jeremy's situation.

"Jeremy is a complete cry for help. His homelife is a wreck. He has never gotten along with his teachers or peers, and he cares nothing about school. Jeremy is not like other kids, and we can't expect him to be. I refuse to give up on him. He's created a spectacle for himself in our school, and we've got to help him rewrite his story before he goes to middle school. If we don't, he will be headed down a lifelong road to failure. He doesn't know how to get himself out of the mess he has created and continues to make. I feel like this is his last chance. We've got to find a way to set him up for success this year."

Jeremy disrupted the entire morning for his teacher and the rest of the class, yet she was still ready to supply him with endless love and grace, and more importantly, the belief that he could make a positive change. She wowed me that day.

That year, Jeremy's teachers and administrators rallied together to help him create a plot twist for his life. Were there tough days along the way? Of course, but with every setback, he took two steps forward. Because of his teacher's leadership, Jeremy formed genuine, renewed relationships with all of his teachers and had a fantastic fifth grade year.

The day we came back to school after Christmas break, I welcomed Jeremy with open arms and told him how happy I was to see him. His response?

"This is the best year I've ever had in school, Mrs. Paschall. I used to get in trouble all the time. My teachers have really helped me learn how to control my emotions better. I actually missed this place over Christmas break!"

Jeremy's life had been redirected because his teacher saw a potential in him that he didn't know existed, and she did whatever it took to unlock it.

I am to the point where I believe that every excuse we make for any child's lack of success is invalid. What a child can or cannot do is rarely a ramification of their capability; rather, it is a result of the belief others had about who they are. As teachers, we must guard against negative thoughts about our students because this is when we form potentially life changing opinions about kids, and our opinions stem from our core beliefs about them. If you believe a child is going to underachieve, you are going to be right. Kids sense and know how we feel about them. Believe that every student can achieve and succeed, and they will begin to believe in their own capabilities.

End the excuses and focus on the solutions. In order to help kids overcome battles, we've got to be there reminding one another that we have the power to change a child's narrative. Kids create messes for themselves from which they don't know how to escape. Rather than continuing to let them be a spectacle for everyone else to see, love them enough to change their story. Don't coddle your coworkers by allowing excuses to creep in when things go awry. That creates toxicity in a school's culture and sends a child's potential into a

> Kids create messes for themselves from which they don't know how to escape. Rather than continuing to let them be a spectacle for everyone else to see, love them enough to change their story.

downward spiral. Build culture by encouraging one another to stay the course and do whatever it takes to multiply excellence. Leaders don't give up on creating plot twists within their students' narratives.

You can either be the educator who gives a student's reputation a life sentence or the one who diverts their pathway. It's up to you. Many kids are on the road to failure because of reasons that are beyond their control. Be the person who redirects their path.

Will You Be My Champion Even When I Do Not Ask?

I believe that the number one reason many kids don't reach success is not because of their circumstances, but because they lack an advocate who is willing to fight for them. How powerful would our world be if every child had a champion, someone who is willing to do whatever it takes to help them overcome their obstacles? It is *always* possible to overcome a tough situation, but sometimes it requires out of the box thinking and not succumbing to the only options you *think* you have from which to choose. Champions don't let circumstances become the excuse for kids not achieving.

Macie's Story

During my first year as an administrator, our school counselor and a teacher informed me about a student named Macie. Macie was adopted when she was a baby, and her parents were in their 70's. Her father had recently suffered two strokes, which left him bedridden and unable to financially support the family. The mother was serving as his caretaker, so she was also unable to work outside of the home. They lost possession of their car because they couldn't make the payments, and they struggled to pay the bills which resulted in their electricity being shut off. To top it all off, they struggled to keep groceries in the house, and they couldn't take the father to his doctor's appointments due to their lack of transportation. Home health wasn't an option either.

One morning, Macie walked into school wearing an expression that was filled with sadness and defeat.

"Good morning, Macie. Is everything ok?"

"My dad fell last night, and my mom couldn't lift him back in bed. She called 9-1-1 to come help her pick him up, but they wouldn't come because it wasn't a medical emergency. I hate seeing my mom cry and my dad in pain. I just want to go home."

Our hearts broke into a million pieces that Macie had been facing such hardships at home for so long. Thankfully, her teacher and counselor recognized the need early on and had already been providing resources such as clothing and food items, but unfortunately, clothing and food bags would only make a small dent in the list of needs Macie's family had. I knew it, and the teachers knew it, but we were at a loss of what else our school could provide. Macie was struggling in every way at school due to her circumstances. She wasn't the only one who needed a champion. Her parents did too, and Macie wouldn't reach success until we found a way to help. Home is where the start is.

Over the Christmas break, I came across a social media post where someone was donating a hospital bed. I called Macie's mom, Mrs. Johnson, and asked if this might be something they needed. She said yes, so my husband and a few friends helped me deliver the hospital bed that night. While we were there, I asked Mrs. Johnson's permission to reach out to community members to see if they could provide some assistance to their family. A church in the community happily jumped at the opportunity and thanked us for making them aware. The following week, church members stopped by their house to make a financial donation. They also set up a schedule for women to visit their house each week and take Mrs. Johnson to run necessary errands. Each week, their church bus now picks Macie up so that she can attend church services every time the doors are open. Because of the school's community,

Macie's family is no longer enduring their hardships alone, and Macie's needs have been met so that she can achieve greater success at school. Recently, Mrs. Johnson called me and left the following voicemail:

"Mrs. Paschall, I just want to thank you for all you've done to help our family. I didn't even know who you were until the day you called me about the hospital bed! We are so grateful. When are you coming back to see us? I'd love to meet your little girl. I'll talk to you soon."

How far are you willing to go to help a child? Will you be someone's champion, even when they do not ask? Don't deceive yourself into thinking the only resources you have to offer are food bags and clothing. You've got an entire community at your back door. Think outside the box. Rally the troops by building a partnership with businesses and churches in the community so you can work together to champion kids and their families. It's all about making connections, and sometimes it's as simple as sending out an email or making a phone call.

Administrators, effective leadership starts at the top. What kind of example are you modeling in your school? Are you a leader who has a relentless, "whatever it takes" mentality to help a child? Or are you a leader who truly believes all you have to offer are the resources within the four walls of your school? What you model is what you will get back in return. Your mentality will trickle down to the rest of your faculty and staff. It doesn't always have to be you doing all the work. Create a culture of synergy in your school's community.

Every obstacle we come across in life allows us an opportunity to improve the circumstances in which we find ourselves. Don't be the educator who sits on the sidelines talking about how unfortunate a situation is. Do something about it, and don't go down without a fight. Kids are depending on us. Be the leader who opens doors for others to use their strengths so that we can multiply excellence by championing kids in immeasurable ways. Be someone's champion, even when they do not ask.

To Champion for Students, We Must Also Champion for Teachers

Teaching is arguably one of the hardest jobs on the planet. We work every day to teach, grade, and plan upcoming lessons for kids, but this list doesn't begin to scratch the surface of all that a teacher's job entails. The toughest part about teaching is facing kids who are suffering from emotional and physical hardships at home that are beyond our control. Constantly serving others can leave us feeling depleted and weighed down. Compassion fatigue is real. What are you doing to make sure your faculty feels supported each day?

The school administrator should energize and inspire a staff more than anyone else. You're the one who is there and in the trenches with them; therefore, you hold the power to have the greatest influence to multiply excellence. While every decision we make should be in the best interest of kids, this doesn't mean the adults don't matter or count. Happy adults lead to happy classrooms. When you build a culture that is rooted with trust, support, and encouragement, it will create a powerful and invaluable ripple effect within the school. It starts with you.

Below is a list of action steps you can take as a leader to create a supportive and healthy culture:

1. "Gotcha!" or "I Got You!" - Which message do you send?
In my years of experience as a teacher, district coach, and school administrator, I have had the opportunity to work with many administrators across the state, all with varying leadership styles. I'll never forget a time I visited classrooms with an administrator when I was an instructional coach. We were still in the first month of school, and I was so excited to see instruction and interact with the kids. When we walked into the first classroom, the administrator immediately walked to the back corner of the room with a notepad and began taking notes. Being brand new to

the job, I wasn't prepared for this, so I followed suit. We stayed in the room for about fifteen minutes, watching instruction from the back corner. We had zero interaction with the kids, and the only interaction I had with the teacher was when I introduced myself as we were walking out. The teacher nervously smiled, but it was obvious she didn't want to carry on a conversation with me. I wanted to crawl in a hole. I felt so uncomfortable during those fifteen minutes, so I can only imagine how the teacher felt, seeing that the two of us had never met. We traveled to more classrooms, and the same pattern continued: we stood in the back corner with a notepad.

The next day, I visited another school. Being more prepared, I let the administrator know up front that I would interact like a student while I was there to make the teacher and students feel comfortable with my presence. As the administrator unlocked the door to the first classroom, he looked back at me, grinned, and said, "Absolutely!" Immediately, he walked in and sat on the floor with a group of kindergarteners who were at their math station and began playing the math game with them. The teacher and students didn't skip a beat. It was obvious this principal did this regularly. The teacher welcomed me and let me know how excited she was to work with me that year. She continued on with her lesson and included us like we were a part of the class, and this pattern continued in the rest of the classrooms we visited. This administrator had created a culture in which teachers felt safe and excited about having visitors in their room. You can't fake that. At the end of the day, a few of the teachers came back to talk with me and asked to schedule a day that I could visit their classrooms again and model a lesson.

How you carry yourself when you enter a teacher's classroom can make or break a culture. As an administrator are you creating a culture of "Gotcha!" or "I Got You!"? Whether it is intentional or not, when you silently walk to the back corner of a classroom, you give teachers the feeling you are trying to catch them doing something wrong. Champion for teachers by making them feel comfortable when you visit their classrooms. When teachers feel supported, they will be open to constructive feedback, coaching, and new learning.

2. Invest Your Time

As the instructional leader in your school, how do you help your teachers grow professionally? Do you decide for them how they need to grow? Or do you empower your teachers by letting them have a vital role in the decision making?

During my first year as an administrator, our first-grade teachers came to me feeling discouraged and defeated about how to teach math. As a grade level, they were struggling. I asked what they felt they needed in order to grow, and they expressed that they wanted to see what a full math block of instruction should look like. That day, I contacted our district math specialist, as well as the strongest first grade math teacher in our school system and arranged for these teachers to observe her instruction. On the day they visited her classroom, I went with them. Together, we watched the lesson and reflected on the things they wanted to bring back to their own classrooms. For the remainder of the day, they collaborated with this first-grade teacher, and she worked with them to plan lessons for the upcoming weeks. Since that day, their math instruction has TRANSFORMED! For the first time in their 15+ years of experience, they are genuinely excited about teaching math. All it took was listening to their needs and finding a way to meet those needs.

Champion teachers by allowing them to visit other schools so they can gather fresh, authentic ideas about how they can grow professionally. Oftentimes, we think the best professional development out there is a workshop. Sometimes it is, but be careful to not "over train" your teachers. There is no better professional development than getting to watch a superstar teacher teach a lesson in real time! Step outside the four walls of your school to learn how much better your school could be. Sometimes, we simply don't know what we don't know. Don't blame teachers for weak instruction if you aren't creating opportunities for enlightenment. It is important that everyone is on the same page with what great instruction looks like. The most important piece to this puzzle is that you, the administrator, visit the school with them. Teachers need to see how invested you are. If you don't invest your time in teachers as they willingly make a change, don't expect the positive changes to stick.

Most teachers have a growth mindset, but unfortunately, many of them are not provided the opportunity to express what they need to grow. Instead, it is decided for them. When this happens, resistance begins to creep in. When teachers feel listened to and supported, they will desire to grow. Champion teachers by **listening** to their needs. **Problem solve** with them, and most importantly, **invest** your time in them as they take strides to make a positive change. Relationships are a key factor in building a positive culture in a school, but how much time you invest in growing your teachers will lead to a culture of excellence.

3. Tune In

On any given day, teachers are counselors, janitors, diagnosticians, curriculum designers, detectives, researchers, engineers, problem solvers, caregivers, and the list goes on. Teachers are so much more than just a teacher, and yet, they still show up each day, ready to take on this Herculean job, regardless of the reality of their own world. Appreciate your faculty and staff, reminding them of their value and worth often.

As we all know, stress levels fluctuate within a school throughout the year. Administrators, it is important that you tune in when stress levels are elevated. Don't turn a blind eye to it. High stress leads to low morale, which can negatively impact the culture within your school.

One year, I could sense that stress levels were high for many of our teachers. We had just received mid-year data, and a few grade levels' data were not where they had hoped. They were working hard to adjust their instruction, which was requiring additional planning time outside of school. Self-criticism and fatigue were written all over their faces, which is the last thing we want for teachers. They are the difference makers. We've got to do whatever it takes to help them remember their value and worth.

One cold and dreary Monday morning in January, my principal and I surprised the teachers with hot coffee and donuts. We went door to door with our coffee cart before school started.

"Good morning, Mrs. Stanley! We've got coffee and donuts this morning for you to counteract this cold and dreary morning. I want you to know how grateful I am for you. You are doing a great job. Thank you so much for all you do each day."

Mrs. Stanley's eyes filled with tears.

"You have no idea how much this means to me. It is so nice to feel appreciated. I spent four hours here on Saturday, and I am feeling down and tired this morning. This is just what I needed to cheer me up before the kids arrive!"

That morning, I received numerous texts and emails from teachers letting me know how much they appreciated the coffee cart.

One of the greatest emotional needs a teacher has is to feel appreciated. Appreciate your faculty and staff and do it often.

Ideas for showing appreciation:

- Write positive notes - There is no greater feeling than receiving handwritten words of affirmation from your boss. It is one of the most impactful things you can do!
- Tell them in person - Let them see your genuiness. Tell them in person how much their hard work means to you!
- Coffee/snack cart - Who doesn't love coffee and snacks early in the morning? Teachers need administrators to be their biggest cheerleader.
- Duty free lunch - If you work in a state where teachers do not receive duty free lunch, this is the cheapest and most wonderful gift you can give a teacher.

- Showcase their hard work on social media.
- Request appreciation letters from families through a Google Form.
- Arrange for community and parent volunteers to wash their cars during the school day.
- Spa Day - Hire a masseuse to spend the day in your teacher's lounge. Set up a water bar with lemons, limes, and berries along with a few salt lamps and essential oils. The teachers will love it.

4. Go to Bat for Teachers

Being a teacher can be overwhelming. Every year, more and more teachers are leaving the educational profession, but why? According to The National Center for Education Statistics, two of the top reasons teachers are seeking a new profession stems from a lack of coaching support and a negative school culture. (Esdal, 2019) Both reasons point to one overarching cause of teacher turnover: **ineffective leadership**. Administrators, what are you doing to set your teachers up for success? How do you support and guide them through their shortcomings? Champion for teachers by fighting for them in the same way we want them to fight for kids.

Years ago, I met Mrs. Gates, a brand-new teacher who was fresh out of college. She was hired the week before school started, and she was so excited to have her first teaching job. Mrs. Gates practically lived at the school in the days leading up to the first day! Her passion and zeal for teaching was exactly what we want every teacher to have.

Mrs. Gates had 29 students in her 5th grade class, with several of the kids needing a significant amount of additional behavioral and emotional support. A few weeks into school, it was written all over Mrs. Gates's face—she was struggling. The passion and zeal she once had was quickly shifting to frustration and defeat. Mrs. Gates was overcome with bitterness due to the stress that was weighing on her, and by January, she was drowning. She had lost all excitement for teaching, and she dreaded going to work each day. She was a different person from the bubbly teacher I met in August. Do you want to know the saddest part about all of this? Mrs. Gates didn't receive any help from an administrator that year—zero advice and zero coaching support. Instead, she was scolded for her lack of management and low test scores.

Thankfully, Mrs. Gates persevered and stuck it out. She entered into her second year of teaching with a renewed energy, perspective, and plan. She killed it in the classroom the following year, all because of her grit and personal desire to grow. I can't help but wonder what her first year of teaching would have been like had the principal provided her targeted support from day one. Like all of us, Mrs. Gates desired to be a great teacher. She simply didn't yet know how. We all need a principal who will champion us by setting us up for success.

Unfortunately, I have been the teacher who stood back and watched another teacher drown during her first year. Even worse, I talked about it with colleagues, and not once did I offer to help. Shame on me for doing that. Not only did my negligence negatively impact the teacher, it also negatively impacted kids. I hope I never let history repeat itself with this mistake. Teachers, champion your fellow teachers! When they are struggling, extend your grace and support. We are all in this really hard thing together.

Do you dismiss or address the needs of others? Don't be the teacher or principal who sits back on the sidelines discussing what teachers are doing wrong. Teachers are people, and all people go through difficult times both personally and professionally at some point in their lives. Go to bat for them. When teachers aren't performing to your standards, communicate this in a way that is full of clarity and grace. Then fight for them by providing the support they need. Champion for teachers in the same way we want teachers to champion for kids.

Champion for ALL

When teachers and students are apathetic, chances are high that a champion hasn't invested in them. One question we always need to come back to is, "Why aren't students/staff engaged?" We won't know until we ask. Work together to address this as a faculty and staff before the apathy spreads. Champion for teachers and students by viewing them as having strengths that need to be tapped into rather than barriers that must be overcome. When you do this, it will lead to a culture that is grounded in the relentless belief that everyone can achieve excellence. Not only does every student deserve a champion, so does every staff member. Never underestimate the value and importance of human connection. Relationships are the gateway to a person's heart, but the amount of time you invest in helping them make a positive change is what really makes the difference. When people feel valued and appreciated, they will feel better about themselves and desire to reach success.

I want to close this chapter by offering three culture-building ideas that a faculty and staff can easily implement. When practices such as these are in place, the belief system within your school that all kids can achieve will solidify.

Culture Builders

1. Culturize By Calling -It is easy to slip into the habit of only contacting parents when it warrants a negative reason such as behavior or academics. We have created a culture across the country where parents cringe whenever the school is calling because it makes them wonder, "What has my child done now?" It is time to change the norm. A key factor to building positive relationships with parents and students is first recognizing and celebrating the positive talents and virtues a child exhibits. Culturize your school by making at least one positive phone call home every single day. Most importantly, let the child make the phone call with you. It only takes one minute to make a positive phone call home, but the impact that it makes on the child and on the parent will last a lifetime.

On the days you have to have a difficult conversation, parents and students will be much more receptive to the feedback when they have confidence that you have their best interest at heart and are working on the same team to help their child succeed.

District administrators, the example starts from the top. Culturize your school system by calling one teacher each day to let them know how much you appreciate the work they are doing. Let them experience first-hand how wonderful it feels to be recognized in such a personal and positive way.

2. Facelift Fridays - Kids deserve to smile the moment they walk into the school every single day. Every Friday, do something above and beyond to make kids smile the moment they arrive at school. Be sure to take pictures and use the hashtag #FaceLiftFridays on Twitter so we can learn new ideas from one another!

Each day, many kids enter our school building weighed down with unfortunate circumstances, and while we don't have the control over their circumstances, we do have the power to redirect the rest of their day. This is a small way to make a big difference. Culturize your school

63

by changing the course of a child's day. Step outside of the box to make kids fall in love with coming to school.

3. Two Note Tuesdays -It is important that teachers feel validated and appreciated, not only by the administrator, but also their colleagues. Every Tuesday, school administrator Jared Paschall has his faculty and staff participate in Two Note Tuesdays where everyone writes two positive notes to other faculty and staff members in the school. It is critical that we let our staff know that we see their hard work and the heart that they share with others. There is something special about receiving a handwritten note. It evokes an entirely different feeling than getting a nicely written email or text. I guarantee you they will appreciate it and you more. Take it to the next level by having students do the same for one another! With each note that you write to someone, you maximize the domino effect toward culturizing your school.

Reflection Questions

1. Think of a student in your classroom/school who is not succeeding in some area. How will you relentlessly champion for this student to help them overcome their interferences?
2. Oftentimes, academic apathy stems from students not being intrinsically motivated in the classroom. Think of a time when your students weren't engaged in the learning and reflect on how you could enhance future learning experiences.
3. The best books we read often include a plot with a major turning point. Think of a student in your school whose narrative desperately needs redirecting. How will you champion this student by creating a plot twist?
4. You have an entire community in your back door. How can you build a stronger partnership with businesses, churches and community members so you can work together to champion kids and their families? Brainstorm specific ways they can help.

CHAPTER 3

Core Principle 2: Expect Excellence

Be Excellent

Remember Chloe from Chapter 1? Chloe wins the award for being the student who taught me the most about compassion, patience, perseverance, and hope. She had only been a student in our school for five months; however, in this short time, she managed to sever her relationship with every one of her teachers. She was my most frequent flyer for office referrals. Chloe was a brilliant, outgoing, and passionate kid, but she had never been taught how to use these traits productively. She was headed down a spiraling path, and statistics pointed toward her eventually being a high school dropout. It terrified me to think about her future.

One morning, Chloe stormed into my office, ready to explode.

"Well hey there, Chloe."

She slumped into the chair with folded arms and pursed lips as she glared out the window.

"Take a few minutes to cool off. Let me when you're ready to talk." I turned on some soft music and didn't say another word. She just needed the gift of time.

Fifteen minutes passed by.

"Ok, I'm ready to talk."

"Great. Before we start, remind me what I always tell you before we have a chat. What is my purpose at school?"

Her eyes filled with tears. With frustration in her voice, she forced these words out:

"To love me no matter what and help me become the best version of myself."

"Exactly. My purpose isn't to just make sure you learn about reading, math, science and history. I'm here to make sure we are shaping **your** future, and some days are going to be harder than others. Today is one of those hard days. Are you willing to stick it out with me?"

"Yes."

"Ok. Now tell me what happened."

Chloe told me about how she had cussed out and screamed at her teacher, Mrs. Payne.

"SHE YELLED AT ME FIRST! AND I HATE IT WHEN PEOPLE YELL AT ME!"

Chloe proceeded to admit that she had caused disruption throughout the entire lesson. While it is never okay to yell at a student, hopefully this helps you to understand Mrs. Payne's level of frustration. Remember when I told you in Chapter 1 that yelling was the only way Chloe knew to respond to conflict? This was a learned, habitual behavior as a result of her homelife. In order to help Chloe, we were going to have to teach her how to productively respond to conflict. After all, it is our actions, not our words that define us. Reaching excellence requires changing habits.

Chloe reflected on how she could have handled the situation differently. It wasn't that she didn't desire to change, rather she knew it was going to take an extreme amount of effort to break her habit.

"Chloe, do you know what tough love means?"

"Oh great. What are you going to make me do?"

"I'm not going to let you go back to class until you talk to your teacher about what triggers your temper in class. And it must be done with a calm, mature approach."

"Nope. I'm not doing it. I don't like expressing my feelings. Not happening."

"Remind me again of my purpose at school."

With her eyes rolled into the back of her head, she said, "You're helping me become the best version of myself."

"You nailed it. I believe in you and love you **this** much, Chloe. I know you can do this."

I explained to her that she could verbally express her frustrations with her teacher, or she could write them down. It was up to her, but I stood firm that she wouldn't return to her classroom until she resolved the issue with Mrs. Payne and made a commitment to make a change.

"Fine. I guess I'll just be in your office forever."

This girl was strong willed, but until this day, she didn't realize she had met her match. I was relentlessly dedicated to awakening the excellence that was deep inside of her. Finally, three hours later, she let me know she was ready. Chloe and I role-played the conversation to make sure she knew how to communicate appropriately. Then I had a conversation with Mrs. Payne to make sure she was brought up to speed.

"I shouldn't have raised my voice at her, Mrs. Paschall. I know I was wrong. I've never had a student who triggers my temper quite like Chloe does."

That afternoon, Chloe and Mrs. Payne resolved their conflict in my office. For the first time, Chloe was able to appropriately communicate her feelings and frustrations.

After listening to Chloe, the teacher responded by saying, "Chloe, I want to apologize to you. I shouldn't have yelled at you like that. I was wrong. You've helped me to see that I need to work on controlling my own temper. We are actually more alike than you may have realized. Maybe we can help each other."

Chloe smiled, reached inside her pocket, and handed the teacher a letter apologizing for how she had treated her the past few months. Neither of us were prepared for her to give Mrs. Payne that letter. Her words were filled with sincerity, and we knew she meant what she said. This was the day we witnessed a turning point with Chloe, and from that day forward, things were remarkably better. Why? Because Chloe and Mrs. Payne committed to working toward excellence together. The best part of this story is that both Chloe and her teacher made themselves vulnerable by admitting to their shortcomings. They held one another accountable as they changed their habits. These are the moments we live for in education, am I right?

When someone challenges you to grow in a certain area, how do you respond? Is your window of vulnerability open and ready to recognize areas of needed improvement, or do you resist the feedback?

Vulnerability is the bridge to change, and changing habits leads to multiplying excellence, within yourself and others. If we aren't excellent, we are mediocre, at best. Before we expect excellence from others, let's make sure we understand its true meaning. Being excellent isn't about being the best, rather it is about holding the desire and grit to constantly reflect and be better.

Are You a Thermostat or a Thermometer?

If you ever have the opportunity to visit Alabama in the dead of winter, you'll certainly gain a sense of humor about its oscillating weather conditions. One day, it's warm and sunny. The following day, our meteorologists are forecasting tornadoes and flash flood warnings, and within hours, every grocery store is sold out of bread and milk. Three days later, we might be building snowmen in the front yard. If only I were exaggerating. Alabama's weather is completely unpredictable during the winter months. Meteorologists have a hard job. There are many days they have to make reactive decisions when sharing the forecast with the public, knowing they will soon be sending thousands of people into panic mode. They are at the complete mercy of the predicted forecast with no control over changing the outcome.

While meteorologists may not have control over regulating the climate, educators do. There are two types of people in a school or school system: **thermometer reporters** and **thermostat adjusters**. The thermometers give an account of the temperature, while the thermostats dynamically regulate it. Whatever role you are in, you are one of the two. There is no in between. How do you respond to the ever-changing culture and climate conditions within your school? Do you proactively regulate the temperature, making small, intentional adjustments to heat and cool the room, or are you merely observing, reporting and reacting to what is happening? Don't deceive yourself into thinking you have to be in a leadership role to be a thermostat adjuster.

During my first year serving as the district math specialist, our curriculum team met with a group of teachers to begin creating new math pacing guides and common assessments so that we could improve our math instruction. Have you ever had one of those days when you confidently begin leading a group of people, and suddenly it all blows up in your face? This was one of those days for me. The teachers were at their boiling point within the first ten minutes, feeling frustrated because they didn't understand why we needed to create new pacing guides and common assessments.

"They are fine the way they are."
"My kids can't do this new math. It's too hard."
"I am so tired of change!"

I was completely caught off guard because I didn't have an accurate measure of the temperature across our district, and as a result, my plan backfired. It would have been so easy to call it a day and report the temperature conditions to my bosses so that they could deal with it. Even worse, I could have forced the teachers to do the work anyway or given in to their frustrations by lowering our expectations of what kids were capable of. But what good would any of that have done?

A lack of teacher investment derives from ineffective leadership.

I needed to find a way to adjust the thermostat in our school system without lowering the standards.

We didn't work on pacing guides and assessments that day. Instead, our curriculum team gathered together to listen to this small group of teachers. They needed to be heard. Over the next month, I traveled from school to school, listening to our teachers' ideas about the best way to enhance math instruction across our district. This approach was received so differently than my previous one. Want to know what we decided upon collectively? We needed new pacing guides and common assessments, as well as instructional support for teachers as they implemented the new practices, which was the exact plan I had all along. Where I went terribly wrong was with my initial approach. Had I gauged the temperature before the initial meeting, I could have developed a strategic and proactive plan to regulate it.

The next time we met to develop pacing guides and assessments, the temperature in the room was vastly different. Momentum was high and the teachers were ready to take the reins. Our teachers ended up creating some of the strongest pacing guides and assessments I have seen. Why? Because they were invested, and the initiative was collective. Leaders who expect excellence find a way to keep the temperature regulated without compromising high standards.

Before you expect excellence from others, be sure you've regulated the climate so all stakeholders are set up to successfully put their best foot forward. Learn from my mistake. Don't be the leader who doesn't even know what the temperature in the room is. Effective teachers and leaders regularly read the temperature in the building. If you aren't taking an accurate temperature, you can't adjust the thermostat.

John Maxwell once said, "Momentum is the greatest of all change agents" (Maxwell, 2005). Oftentimes, this is the missing link in maintaining a positive climate and culture. In order to keep the temperature regulated, you must generate the momentum *before* you make a change. Allow these changes to happen in increments. Don't try to shoot the thermostat up 20 degrees. It isn't about speed; it is about momentum. Gauge the temperature, and lead with a positive and interdependent mindset. Go slow at first to go fast later. When momentum is high, it is amazing how many things can be accomplished.

Seek Excellence

Excellence. What does this word really mean in the world of education?

A Google search of "excellence" includes definitions such as "the quality of being outstanding" (Merriam-Webster, n.d.), but how do we get a true measure of this in our schools? In my years of working in an administrative role, I have asked many teachers and administrators to give an overall rating on a scale of 1-10 on how they feel that they (or their schools) are doing in this area. More often than not, they rank themselves higher than the reality based on all available evidence, but why?

I believe this false reality stems from the fact that all we know is what we have seen inside the four walls of our classroom or school. When we don't actively seek opportunities to learn new ideas, we will have a fragmented understanding of what excellence could look like.

The truth is that we are never really done reaching excellence. Education is ever-changing, so our definition of excellence should be also. We only know what we know. It's essential that teachers and administrators branch out to gain ideas on how to constantly be better.

Here are some critical ways that we should work toward reaching excellence:

1. Grow Your Network

When I entered into my first year as an assistant principal, I quickly realized that I was on an island. No one else in my school was in the same role as me, and there were only three other elementary assistant principals in my school system. I was craving a network of people with whom to exchange ideas.

During the first week of school, my friend Adam Welcome (co-author of *Kids Deserve It*) called me to see how my first week was going as a new assistant principal. Toward the end of our conversation he challenged me to build a network for elementary assistant principals across the country.

"People across the country are in the same boat as you, Emily. Change that, not only for you, but for everyone else."

I accepted the challenge and made a post on Twitter the following day announcing that I had formed a Voxer group for any elementary assistant principals who wanted to be a part of this. Within hours, hundreds of people from across the world were asking to join, and since then, we have formed a tight-knit community where we have safe, ongoing conversations filled with advice and fresh ideas for one another. I wouldn't be anywhere near the administrator I am today without the #ElemAPNetwork. They challenge me to reach a level of excellence that I never could have imagined myself.

2. Read

Reading is one of the easiest and most impactful ways to gain new ideas. There are hundreds of educational books out there, ranging from classroom instruction to educational leadership. Read books by yourself, as well as with your colleagues. Book studies are essential for collectively moving a school forward. There really is no excuse to not read. Sharpen your definition of excellence by picking up a new book.

3. Step Outside the Four Walls of Your School

We do not do enough of this. This is one of the most impactful ways educators can be inspired to make a positive change. Below are just a few reasons to bring teachers and parents to visit other schools:

- Help your PTO/PTA network with officers in other schools to gain new ideas for raising and spending money for your school.
- Allow teachers to visit other schools to observe other teachers during instruction. Oftentimes this is the greatest professional development we can offer teachers.
- Visit other schools with your Leadership Team as a way to collectively discover new ways to take your school to new heights.
- Need to give the interior of your school a face-lift? Allow teachers and parents to visit other schools to gather fresh ideas.

Administrators, it is essential that you also step outside of the four walls of your school. When you don't, you're modeling the status quo instead of a quest for ongoing excellence. What you model is what you will get back in return. If you want your school to reach excellence, you've got to be willing to step out and discover what that greater excellence could be.

4. Hire for Excellence

Hiring is one of the most critical responsibilities of a school administrator. Who you hire has the potential to shift your culture in one of two directions. Kids can't afford for us to settle for average when we hire. Set your expectations high in the hiring process. Have a process in place that trains your faculty and staff how to go through the interview procedures when they are on a selection team. Always, always, always have teacher candidates teach a lesson. Many people can kill it in an interview. Find out who can kill it when teaching kids before you add them to your staff.

5. Welcome Coaching Support

Seek out the people who will tell it to you straight, regardless of whether you want to hear it. Sometimes we just need someone there to help us see things through a different lens. Seeking honesty and transparency is one of the greatest ways we can become better versions of ourselves. In my years of experience, I have known this to be the most resisted avenue for growth by both teachers and administrators. Whether you have been in education for 3 or 30 years, if you are resistant to having a mentor or coach, ask yourself why. If the words, "I don't need" pop into your head, chances are high that you may need it the most.

Our definitions of excellence will vary, depending on the opportunities we've taken to discover new levels of excellence. If you're only using examples inside your school to define excellence, it is likely that your definition lines up with the status quo. Don't fall prey to this. Our kids deserve better. If you want to be excellent, you must be hungry for it. Seek excellence so that you can multiply it. Benchmark against the best, learn from the best, and believe that it can be done!

Stay in the Trenches

As administrators, it is easy for us to fall out of touch with what it was once like to be a classroom teacher. Additionally, when we become administrators, we are suddenly leading a group of people who work in roles we've never actually experienced ourselves, such as bus drivers, receptionists or instructional assistants. What are you doing to better understand their perceptions? As we expect excellence, let's make sure we take opportunities to understand what it is like to be in their shoes:

1. Feel Their Pain

When I became an assistant principal, I quickly realized how unprepared I was for bus safety and bus discipline. I felt like I was constantly putting out fires during the first two months of school and felt frustrated because I couldn't figure out why there were so many bus issues. I met with our drivers one afternoon and expressed to them that I wanted to start riding their buses to better understand how I could help. After riding the first bus, I quickly learned the root cause behind our bus issues: **ineffective leadership.**

Our bus drivers were great. They weren't the problem. The issue was that I hadn't comprehended the difficulty of their job or how to help, and I would never have truly understood it until I jumped in the trenches by riding the bus with them. Many of our students were a huge distraction on the bus, and this was due to the fact that I had not supported our drivers on the front end by establishing expectations. After that day, my principal and I met with the bus drivers to form clearer expectations, not only of the drivers and students, but also of the administrators. On that day, I made the commitment to ride every bus at least once each semester.

Bus issues were minimal from that day forward and my relationships with the drivers grew exponentially. The drivers taught me that the bus is one of the best places to build relationships with kids. I now surprise the students by riding a random bus every Friday morning, and it is one of my favorite things to do. You never know what you will learn when you get in the trenches. Our bus drivers are the first and last ones to see many of our students each day. Some spend six or more years with these kids and have the opportunity to make a tremendous impact on kids' lives. Let's be sure to give them the honor and support they deserve.

When we expect excellence from others, let's take a walk in their shoes so we can understand their pain and frustrations before developing a plan for improvement.

2. Be a Doer, Not a Teller

Do you challenge the status quo, or do you *change* it? There is a large variance between the two. If we want to change the status quo, teachers need to witness an investment from the top. Telling others how they can be better is very different from working with them to become better. Effective leaders are doers, not tellers. Be a part of the change you are trying to make.

> Telling others how they can be better is very different from working with them to become better.
>
> ∼

I became an administrator at thirty-one years old. Our school was filled with a veteran staff with very low turnover, and many of the teachers were old enough to be my parent. Out of 40 teachers, only 5 of them had fewer than 10 years of experience. If I wasn't careful, I knew my age could easily become a barrier to successfully leading our school. There was a particular grade level of teachers who were unreceptive to me during the first few months of school. And you know what? That is okay. We cannot take things like that personally. Relationships don't always magically form overnight, and it is our responsibility as leaders to find a way to connect with them and build their trust. In order to gain credibility, my approach toward expecting excellence was going to have to be strategic, collective, and filled with service.

At mid-year, our student learning data showed that students were not making adequate progress in reading in the majority of our grade levels. I scheduled a planning day with each grade level so that we could problem solve together how to improve instruction. The day had come where I was meeting with the group of teachers I had not yet formed a strong connection with, and for the first hour of the day, there was a thick air of resistance in the room. I listened to their concerns, frustrations, and thoughts on why they felt their data had regressed. Once they determined where they felt the gaps were in their instruction, *we* developed a targeted plan of what *we* were going to work on that day.

That's right. Hear me loud and clear.

We.

Not them.

WE.

WE spent the rest of the day developing targeted lessons for their upcoming reading unit together. That night, I received an email from three of those teachers thanking me for my support.

One of the messages read:

"Thank you! Thank you! Never in my thirteen years of teaching have I ever had an administrator sit down in the trenches and write lessons with me! I really appreciate your help today and am excited to implement these ideas in my classroom. I'm sorry I unloaded my frustration this morning!"

After that day, my relationship with these teachers was vastly different. Why? Because they knew I was equally invested in students. This sent a clear message that these were *our* kids, not just *their* kids, and I was willing to do whatever it took to help them.

If you are merely sitting on the sidelines and telling teachers what needs to be done to improve, you're sending one of two distinct messages to your staff:

1. It isn't that important to you.

OR

2. You aren't a team player.

Change is hard, and at times it can be painful. In order to make positive changes that stick, leaders must be part of the change. Get in the trenches and do the work.

3. Hold on to Your Craft

As educators, our sole responsibility is to shape kids' futures by loving them no matter what and helping them become the best version of themselves. That being said, it is critical that we always keep "the main thing, the main thing," with the "main thing" being student learning.

One of the most critical roles of an administrator is to be an instructional leader. Principals should be regularly engaged in curriculum, assessment, and pedagogy in ways that are obvious to everyone; however, the most important thing is that a principal never stops teaching. How can we ask teachers to constantly improve their teaching practices if we haven't actually taught a lesson ourselves in years? Does this mean we have to be the best teacher in the building? Absolutely not. But we should always be the lead learner. The best way to portray how important instruction is to us is by holding on to our craft of teaching. Don't ask anyone to do anything you aren't willing to do yourself. Co-teach with a teacher. Teach an intervention group. Model a lesson. Be sure you are regularly sending the message that you're equally invested in helping all kids reach academic success.

It's not just about getting in the trenches, it's about staying there. Principals who don't do this don't know how to help their faculty and staff grow. In order to regulate the thermostat and sustain a change, you've got to stay in the trenches, not as a "gotcha" tactic, but to let your faculty and staff know that you are their biggest supporter.

Broken Window

Years ago, I had the opportunity to visit the Biltmore Estate in North Carolina. The day I was there, workers were replacing a broken window in the front of the mansion. Here I was getting to view what is considered to be the most elegant building in America, and all I could do was zero in on that window. My eyes couldn't see past it. Regardless of how elegant a building may be, a single broken window can cause distraction and take away from its true beauty.

Every school has metaphorical broken windows. Some pop up suddenly, while others may have been abandoned for years. What are the broken windows in your school? Do teachers walk past each other in the hallways without speaking? Are the hallways bare, waiting to be filled with student work? Maybe your front receptionist doesn't receive phone calls with friendliness and warmth. The important thing is that you recognize these "broken windows" and find a productive way to repair them so that they don't make a negative impact on your school's culture.

Consider the following scenario that took place in an elementary school where the counselor was bringing a new 1st grade student and his mother to meet the student's new teacher:

Counselor: Mrs. Edgemont, this is Henry and his mom, Mrs. Adams. Their family just moved here from California. He is going to be a new student in your class.

Teacher: Hi Henry. Hi Mrs. Adams. It is really nice to meet both of you! My name is Mrs. Edgemont.

Teacher: (In an aside to the counselor) Are you sure I am the next person on the list to get a new student? I have 24 students and Mrs. Brown only has 22.

Counselor: Yes ma'am! I told Henry what a great time he is going to have in your classroom. Mrs. Adams let me know that he will be a bus rider each day and that he will usually bring his own lunch.

Teacher: Thank you. I will make sure he gets on the right bus this afternoon.

Imagine the look on the parent and child's face when the teacher's first words to this family was that she wasn't next on the list to get a new student. When word got back to the administrator about what had happened, he had a private conversation with the teacher to prevent this from happening again, but guess what? History repeated itself a few weeks later with another teacher. Why? Because rather than replacing the broken window, he tried to patch it up.

If you are an administrator, how would you have handled this? If you are a teacher, how would you expect your administrator to handle it? While I believe having a conversation with the teacher was warranted, it's important we first ask ourselves this question: Has a process been clearly established and communicated on the front end about how we should greet new students? If the answer is no, you've got a potential broken window in your school. At the next faculty meeting, the administrator presented the above script to the faculty and had them discuss it in pairs. He posed these three questions for discussion:

1. How do you think this made the student feel?
2. How do you think this made the parent feel?
3. What kind of image might this response send about our school?

After some rich discussion, the faculty developed a process for how to greet new families. The best part about this story is that everyone was able to have a positive, reflective conversation about this. The administrator didn't have to come in and scold the teachers. He simply posed the scenario for the teachers to reflect upon. The outcome? The school now has a fluid, coherent process in place where everyone goes above and beyond to greet new students. The broken window is repaired, and chances are very high that no one will break that window again.

Reflect on the broken windows in your school. What steps are you taking to repair them? Trying to build school culture without coherence is like building a house without blueprints—both scenarios produce poor results. Communication is a key ingredient in forming an excellent school culture. If you haven't communicated clear processes and expectations of excellence, don't expect to see it. A process needs to be put in place, and it must be implemented collectively as one staff.

Sending a blanket email will not fix the broken window. When administrators send blanket emails to address a culture issue, they are sending the message that it wasn't really that important to begin with.

Blanket emails:

1. Cause information overload.
2. Lack a personal touch.
3. Are often overlooked. Why? Because teachers are busy!
4. Cause confusion and misunderstanding.
5. Send the message of authoritarian decision making rather than shared leadership.

The funny thing is, broken windows actually make us work harder than we would have if we had a clear process in place to begin with. Broken windows are culture killers, plain and simple. Some cause animosity amongst staff members, while others send a negative impression to outsiders. Don't be the leader who takes the easy road by just patching up the hole, or worse, sweeping the issue under the rug. Address your broken windows with intentionality so that they don't become an eyesore and distract others from the great things happening in your school.

Assume Positive Intent

Picture this:

You walk into Mrs. Holcomb's classroom in the middle of her math block. The kids are sitting in silence as they listen to the teacher deliver the day's lesson through a lecture format. Heads are down on the desk and there is zero excitement for learning. Mrs. Holcomb's students are way underperforming year after year. At a professional development training, you'll find her sitting in the back of the room, appearing to be uninterested in the learning opportunity, and she never speaks up or asks a question. In a data meeting, she is full of excuses, and it's nearly impossible to get her to reflect on the true root cause of her data.

What are your initial thoughts about Mrs. Holcomb? She's lazy? She needs to go to the house? She doesn't care about kids?

When I was a district math specialist, I was asked to coach Mrs. Holcomb. "Seriously?" I thought. "What's the point?" Immediately, thoughts of dread and frustration consumed my mind, feeling like this was going to be a lost cause. "How can you help a teacher who doesn't care to learn?" The night before our first meeting, I came across this quote while scrolling through my Twitter feed:

"Assume positive intent."

Timing is an interesting thing. This was the exact message I needed to read to get my mindset in check. When teachers are resistant, it's typically not because they are insubordinate. There is always a reason for their reluctance. I had never worked with this teacher before, yet I still cast judgment on her before I gave her a chance. She deserved to be given the benefit of the doubt. She deserved to be heard. And most importantly, she deserved grace.

Anytime I begin a coaching cycle with teachers, our first meeting is always centered around getting to know one another. I love to learn about why they became a teacher, who they admire, their strengths, and the areas in which they feel they need to grow. My first meeting with Mrs. Holcomb was uncomfortable. Her walls were up, resistance in the air was thick, and she avoided my question about where she felt she needed to grow as a teacher. I had to find a way to work that question in three times until she finally gave this true and honest answer:

"Ok. I'm going to be completely honest with you. I don't know anything about these new math standards. They make no sense to me. This isn't the way I learned growing up. I am so intimidated by this coaching cycle. I don't want you to think I don't care. I'm overwhelmed, and I just don't understand."

You see, it wasn't that she didn't care. It wasn't that she was lazy. She was insecure. And she allowed her insecurities to become a roadblock to excellence.

I spent the rest of our time together listening to her as she talked through her insecurities. It's amazing how quickly a person's body language and attitude can change when you help them safely uncover their true barrier toward excellence. For the remainder of the semester, Mrs. Holcomb and I formed a special bond as we worked together to learn the best way to teach her students. It was nothing short of awesome to see her fall in love with teaching again. At the end of the school year, her students moved from 44% to 80% proficiency in math. Her "why" behind why she went into education in the first place had been revived, and her teaching transformed as a result of it.

Until proven otherwise, we should **always** begin with assuming positive intent. You will be amazed by how much it changes your initial approach to a situation. We're all human, and change is never easy. Most teachers are doing the best they know *how* to do, and they believe what they are doing is good teaching. Some people are resistant to change because they are afraid this approach is not going to work, while others allow insecurity to creep in because they don't know how to put the new learning into practice. As leaders, we've got to be willing to get into their skin and understand their perspective. Why are they this way? Rather than making assumptions about their reality, let's ask questions to understand where they are coming from.

While assuming positive intent should always be our initial approach, it shouldn't ever change our expectations of excellence. When we seek first to understand a person's current reality, we are more likely to open their window of receptivity and their inner desire to reach new heights. It's important to keep in mind that we should only assume positive intent up to the point where it's not smart anymore. Don't be the fool who continues to get burned. If someone continues to take advantage of a situation or refuses to make a change, you have evidence to support the fact that you need to take a different approach.

The point is, so many times, we don't approach a situation by giving the benefit of the doubt. Instead, we project ideas and opinions that were never true to begin with and turn the person off from ever wanting to make a positive change. Assuming positive intent is always a better starting point. You will be amazed by how it changes your whole approach to any situation.

> The point is, so many times, we don't approach a situation by giving the benefit of the doubt. Instead, we project ideas and opinions that were never true to begin with and turn the person off from ever wanting to make a positive change. Assuming positive intent is always a better starting point.

Academic Excellence

Regardless of your role in education, to what extent do you consider yourself an instructional leader? On a scale from 1-10, how would you rate yourself in leading your classroom, school, or district toward academic excellence? Do your students, staff, and district leaders have a common focus? How are you setting others up for success to reach exemplary status for themselves? Without a common vision, it's easy for our focus to become discombobulated with all the things we try to put into practice at one time:

Data meetings.

Teacher observations.

Instructional rounds.

Schoolwide strategic plans.

Professional development.

The list is endless.

Do you view all of these processes as a vital component of what it takes to culturize a classroom, school, or district? Or do you feel like each of these are just one more thing to check off of your list? Are you a manager or leader? While strong management is a key element to a successful school day, this alone won't culturize your environment. Leadership is defined not by how you manage an institution, but by how you influence and guide the talents and energies of everyone around you. Instructional leadership starts at the top. It doesn't start with your instructional coach. It doesn't start with peers. It starts with you!

Every staff member should arrive at school each day ready to work as hard as we would during the first week of school. If you truly want all kids to reach greatness, it is essential that you create a culture where the ones in your charge are driven to produce their best work, sparking intrinsic motivation and productive perseverance every day. That isn't too much to ask or expect. Remember, mediocrity kills culture. Understand, however, that putting expectations of excellence into motion takes strategy and intentionality. It is critical you communicate and expect excellence in a way that sets others up for success.

Consider the following scenarios. As you read, reflect on your journey thus far as an instructional leader.

Scenario 1:

In October, *School A* held their first-grade level data meetings of the year to analyze mid-semester data. It was discovered in these meetings that students were not making adequate academic progress. There was a level of discomfort and disappointment during the meeting, but no one knew the root cause, nor did they know what the next steps should be. By default, the principal then had each teacher select target students to focus on for the remainder of the semester, but there was no discussion about needed areas of instructional growth. The following week, the principal did walkthrough observations in hopes that it would put pressure on the teachers, and in turn, improve data. Later that day, she sent the teachers a blanket email with a list of glows and grows. "Check! Mark that off the list," she thought. January rolls around, and once again, it's time to assess student learning. Just as the data showed in October, the students were still making inadequate progress. At the January data meetings, the principal's frustration level toward the teachers grew. "Not even the target students made sufficient improvement," she thought. In the following weeks, she reactively turned up the heat by doing weekly walkthroughs, hoping this would cause teachers to take their data more seriously. The teachers grew frustrated and morale began to plummet. The teachers were working hard and felt unappreciated for their efforts. They wanted their data to improve just as much as their principal did, but they didn't know how to fix it. Sadly, their principal didn't either.

Scenario 2:

In August, *School B* held a school wide data meeting to proactively help teachers discover needed areas of growth as one school. Together, they discovered a weaker area in their instructional core that would be their central focus for the entire year. Their problem of practice was, "How can we incorporate more high cognitive tasks into our instruction to enhance student engagement?" For two school years, all instructional action steps were centered around this idea. Why? Because they needed this much time to gain a collective understanding of what a high cognitive task looks like. The faculty made a yearly plan of action steps to ensure everyone was making continuous instructional improvement.

Teachers received professional development centered around this idea. They were given opportunities to visit classrooms to watch a high cognitive task in action. When administrators conducted teacher evaluations, they communicated that they would be looking through this lens so they could gauge how their teachers were growing in this area. Teachers visited each other's classrooms to collect data in real time on how they were doing with this focus as a school. At mid-year data meetings, teachers discovered that there was a subgroup of kids that wasn't progressing at an appropriate rate. Rather than the principal reactively assuming administrative walkthroughs were a solution, he gave teachers the support needed to figure out the root cause. Because this school had a common vision, instructional practices grew by leaps and bounds over those two years, and as a result, students made tremendous academic progress.

Which scenario best describes your school, based on your previous practices as an instructional leader? Do you lead with focus and take proactive, strategic measures to increase student achievement? Or do you lead without a collective long-term vision and default to reactive responses when student learning isn't progressing? It is critical that you begin your year by working with your teachers to develop an academic focus that everyone can improve upon for the entire school year. Based on your data, what is a necessary area of improvement in your instructional core? Once you establish this collectively, everything you do to improve student learning should be centered around this academic focus. On the next page, you will find a diagram that shows the cycle of how to reach academic excellence.

Begin by analyzing your data to understand your school's current reality. Choose an area of focus and make a detailed plan describing how you will work together to improve. Communicate on the front end that you will monitor instructional progress through observations, data meetings, and learning walks. Sudden, unexpected mid-year walkthroughs are never the answer to achieving academic excellence. This

DETERMINE THE WHAT
Professional Development & Coaching Support

What professional learning is necessary to help us accomplish our problem of practice? How will we plan for professional development and measure its effectiveness? How will we determine which teachers will need a coaching cycle? How will we measure the effectiveness of the coaching cycles?

Cycle of Academic Excellence:
What is our academic focus?

ANALYZE AND REFLECT ON RESULTS
Teacher Observations, Data Meetings & Learning Walks

Teacher Observations: How will you collect evidence of student learning during classroom observations? How will you communicate progress and areas of growth to individual teachers?

Data Meetings: How often will you hold data meetings? What data will you use to measure progress? What questions will you ask to help teachers reflect on the data? What are the next instructional steps?

Learning Walks: How will you plan for teachers to visit one another's classrooms to look for evidence of your school's academic focus implemented? How will teachers collect evidence of student learning? What conversations will you all have about the data? How will this data be used to make further decisions about classroom instruction?

PROVIDE THE HOW
Classroom Visits and Planning Time

Professional development gives the 'what'. School visits show the 'how'. How will you arrange for teachers to see your school's academic focus action in other schools? (Oftentimes this is the most impactful but most frequently forgotten professional development.) How will you arrange for grade levels to have additional planning time to work toward achieving your school's academic focus and vision?

will kill a school's culture. Reactive responses only send teachers into panic mode to teach harder, but if their instructional practices aren't excellent to begin with, what good will teaching harder do? Sometimes, teachers don't know how to be better. Instead, send the message "I Got You!" as you work together to achieve academic excellence. Never lower your expectations. People will rise to what you clearly communicate and expect. Be the instructional leader who multiplies excellence by influencing and guiding the talents and energies of everyone around you to reach exemplary teaching status.

Embrace Difficult Conversations

Recently, my car started making a noise that just didn't sound right. I felt like the brake pads might need to be changed, but after a few days, the noise faded. (This is also the part of the story where I should admit that I thoroughly enjoy singing along to loud music in the car, so it could be that I drowned the sound out, but I digress.) A couple of months went by, and suddenly my car began making an embarrassingly loud screeching sound whenever I put the slightest pressure on the brakes. After receiving many stares from concerned drivers around me, I took it as a telltale sign that I needed to take my car to the shop. The mechanic confirmed that I needed new brake pads, and he also revealed that I needed new rotors because I had worn my brake pads all the way down to the metal. You can imagine the extra chunk of change I had to fork over because of my procrastination. The realization that I could have avoided this extra cost had I not ignored the original issue punched me right in the gut.

Unfortunately, this same logic is exercised by many leaders when it comes to having a difficult conversation with someone. Instead of initiating what could have been a simple conversation, we ignore it, which then leads to greater problems in the future. The key to having a difficult conversation is to stop making them difficult. Whether it is an issue of professionalism, toxicity, or underperformance, there comes a time when you must break the silence and embrace the conversation. Avoiding it will lead to broken windows in your school while simultaneously impacting the environment and productivity in a negative way.

Teachers regularly have to confront students to address wrong behaviors or not meeting expectations. Teachers must also wade into the uncomfortable parent conversations. Learning how to have these conversations, instead of avoiding them, makes life easier, and more importantly, it is what is best for kids.

One of the most difficult conversations to endure is when you're in the presence of a resistant employee. It is easier to approach someone when they have blatantly violated a policy than it is to confront an employee who is doing the basics of their job by coming to work on time and meeting fundamental guidelines, however, they still aren't doing their best job for kids. When a person uses resistant language to avoid the reality, how do you handle this? How do you respond in a way that guides them to self-reflect rather than having to react with harsh words?

When I transitioned from being a classroom teacher to working in an administrative role with adults, I quickly learned that there are many people who don't think they need help, and I didn't know how to productively respond to that. This was frustrating for me. No matter how logically I presented an idea, there were still those who would respond with resistance. I viewed these people as stubborn, lazy, and unreasonable. My natural response was to become more assertive with the point I was trying to make, which got me nowhere. How wrong I was. What I failed to understand was that I had not invested enough time in helping them grow by allowing them to reflect on their own actions.

Peter Block's book *Flawless Consulting* (Block, 2000) has been a valuable source for me as it has helped me to understand how to appropriately respond to resistance. Block describes resistance as a natural and emotional reaction against the process of being helped (Block,

2000). For the remainder of this section, I hope to give a synopsis of what I took away from Block's writing and share how it has helped me to become more successful in leading adults.

First and foremost, it is important that you don't allow yourself to take resistance personally. Resistant people are struggling with themselves, not with you. It is difficult to confront the truth when you know you are going to have to make a difficult change that you have actively been trying to avoid. Resistance is natural. Why? Because change is hard for many people; but change isn't a bad thing. We all need to make changes in our life. It is the only way we can grow. What's important is that you are honest with them and support them as they make the change.

Secondly, resistance comes in many forms. Some are very subdued and ambiguous. Other forms of resistance are much easier to spot. When approaching a difficult conversation, it is important that you are able to identify when resistance is taking place so that you know how to properly respond. The chart below is adapted from Peter Block's work and shows some ways resistance could take place in schools:

The Faces of Resistance:

When the Resistance Takes this Form	Name It by Making this Statement
Teacher/parent avoids responsibility for the problem or the solution: They make excuses for themselves or their child.	You don't see yourself as part of the problem.
Flooding you with detail: The teacher/parent gives you more and more information, which you understand less and less.	You are giving me more detail than I need. How would you describe it in a short statement?
Teacher/parent gives one-word answers	You are giving me very short answers. Could you say more?

When the Resistance Takes this Form	Name It by Making this Statement
Teacher/parent continues changing the subject	The subject keeps shifting. Could we stay focused on one area at a time?
Compliance: This is one of the most difficult forms to recognize because you are getting agreement and respect. When the teacher/parent doesn't express reservations to you about the given course of action, it is possible these reservations will come up later in a more damaging way.	You seem willing to do anything I suggest. I can't tell what your real feelings are.
Silence: This is the toughest of all forms. Silence never means consent. Don't fall for this.	You are very quiet. I don't know how to read your silence.
Press for Solutions: "Don't talk to me about problems. I want to hear solutions." The impulse for solutions can prevent the parent/teacher from reflecting or learning anything about the essence of the problem.	It's too early for solutions. I'm still trying to find out...
Attack: Red face, angry words, slamming fists - When a parent/teacher attacks, the key is to not take this personally.	You are really questioning a lot of what I do. You seem angry about something.
Intellectualizing and spinning great theories Spinning theories is a way of taking the pain out of the situation.	Each time we get close to deciding what to do, you go back to developing theories to understand what is happening.

When the Resistance Takes this Form	Name It by Making this Statement
Confusion: When you have to explain something two or three times, and the teacher/parent still claims to be confused, this could be their way of resisting.	You seem very confused about what we are discussing. Are you confused about the problem or just not sure what to do about it?
Low energy, inattention	You look like you have other things on your mind and have low energy for this project.

Below is an overview of Block's step by step process for handling the previously stated forms of resistance:

Step 1: Identify in your own mind the form of resistance that is taking place.

Step 2: State, in a nonjudgmental and nonthreatening way to the employee the resistance that is taking place. In other words, name the resistance. Put it into words for the employee to hear.

Step 3: Go silent. This is the hardest part because it's the part where we want to keep on talking to remove the tension. Whatever you do, don't save them. Tension is okay. Let the employee have time to process and respond to your statement about the resistance. This is a critical, and often pivotal part of the confrontation.

Consider the following scenario:

An administrator is meeting with a veteran first grade teacher whose students are underperforming year after year. The teacher has been a broken record with her excuses for years.

Administrator: Let's take a look at your data. I noticed that your students were at 65% benchmark at the beginning of this school year, and now your class is at 36% benchmark. What do you feel is causing this regression?

Teacher: Homelife! The kids don't care, and neither do their parents. No matter how hard I teach, they just don't pay attention. I've got five students who are severely ADHD. On top of that, four of my students have an IEP and three students are English Language Learners. I had Johnny's brother a few years ago and he was low, too. Marisol's mom went to school with me and she was just like Marisol—she didn't care about school. The apple doesn't fall far. I can't get any of the parents to work with them at home. I've tried everything. Six students are going to the interventionist, others are receiving ELL services, and I'm sending extra work home. I don't know what else to do.

(Forms of resistance: Avoiding responsibility and flooding with detail—If you're in a situation where the employee exhibits multiple faces of resistance, choose the one that seems to be a greater concern.)

Administrator: What I'm hearing you say is that you believe the main issue is that the kids and parents don't care. In addition, because you have students with ADHD, learning disabilities, and language barriers, you feel this is also what is causing the regression in your data?

Teacher: Yes, that is correct.

Administrator: So, what I am hearing you say is that you don't see yourself as a part of the problem.

(Teacher begins to stir, making less eye contact.)

Teacher: Well I don't know about that. I was just wanting you to see what I've been up against. This has been my hardest year of teaching in my entire career. No matter what I do, the kids just won't try. I can't even get them to turn their work in. This morning, only half of my class turned in their homework. I don't know what I'm supposed to do if the parents or kids won't put forth any effort.

Administrator: I hear what you're saying, but I want to come back to my previous statement. Based on my observations, what I am hearing you say is that you don't see yourself as a part of the problem.

Teacher: I guess I am, but I don't think you understand what I'm up against.

Administrator: When students don't make adequate academic progress, as educators, we are always a factor to the problem. If we don't see ourselves as a part of the problem, we can't be a part of the solution.

It wasn't until the administrator repeated the statement for the third time about being a factor to the problem that the teacher began to stop avoiding the reality. Tension was thick, but this was the pivotal moment that led to the teacher reflecting upon the changes she needed to make to better help her students. The administrator and teacher set goals together on what the teacher would work on for the remainder of the semester. The goals and expectations were clear before the meeting ended, and the administrator explained how she would follow-up to look for improvement. Most importantly, the administrator gave assurance that she was there to support the teacher along the way as she made these positive and pivotal changes.

One of the most valuable gifts we can give to others is the gift of honesty. Our influence is even more substantial when we invest in our employees in a truthful and kind way that supports their growth and success. When you avoid a difficult conversation that could lead to a better educational pathway for kids, you're sending the message that you don't care. Honest and caring feedback, ongoing support, and patience is always the better option. Embrace difficult conversations. When teachers know better, they do better. And when they do better, you will feel better. Don't let your fears get in the way of doing what's best for kids.

Multiply

When I was hired as the district math specialist in my school system, I stepped into a newly created position. No one else had ever served in this role, and we didn't have any other math coaches in our system. It was just me—responsible for figuring out how to carry math instruction to the next level in nine elementary schools. I felt so intimidated by this when I was hired. How could a single person make such an impact across an entire system? The answer was simple—I couldn't. My first year was a struggle because I had to learn this the hard way. I felt like a first-year teacher all over again. It was a year of putting out constant fires, coaching as many teachers as possible, leading ongoing content training, all while staying afloat with emails and meeting deadlines. This is the short list. You can imagine the late hours I was putting in at night. My bosses were wonderful. They didn't expect this of me. I put the pressure on myself.

Did I make an impact? I sure hope so, but with this approach, it would never be significant. Why? Because I was trying to do it all on my own.

Multiply.

This is the word that slapped me in the face one day as I was wrapping up one of my especially exhausting days.

Multiply.

Multiply a relentless passion for kids.
Multiply exemplary instruction in classrooms.
Multiply support systems for all teachers.
Multiply excellence.

I couldn't do it on my own, and I needed to stop trying. First of all, I was killing myself. Secondly, and most importantly, excellence already existed in our system, and it was at my fingertips. Why wasn't I taking opportunities to multiply their talents?

I began asking myself these questions:

How can I enhance our culture where we work together to multiply excellence so that we can make a greater impact on kids' futures? How can I enhance our culture where we equip one another with the tools that would be helpful in the process of reaching excellence?

As I was nearing the end of my first year in this role, things finally began to click with me. I needed to put a structure in place where everyone was set up to reach their next individualized level of excellence. Excellence comes in all different shapes, levels, and forms. Multiplying excellence isn't just for the super gifted and talented teachers. It is for *all* teachers, ranging from those who are fresh out of college, those who have lost their way, and those who are knocking it out of the park.

The following year, I began spending much of my time in a professional learning community format. I wanted to be able to reach a greater number of teachers at one time, as well as create opportunities for teachers to network with one another. When I created these grade level PLCs, I was very intentional about who I invited. There was always a mix of superstar teachers, those who needed extensive support, and teachers who were new to the profession. I was also intentional about including a mix of positive and negative personality types. Just like in the classroom, it's critical that you pick people who will help one another in a collaborative group. You always want the positive energy to outweigh the negative. Each PLC group consisted of 10-12 teachers, all from the same grade level, but from a mix of schools.

We spent the morning observing one of our high performing teachers teach a full math block. Afterward, the teachers had the opportunity to debrief with the observed teacher and ask questions about the lesson. This typically led to the observed teacher leading an impromptu content training for the PLC team, answering their questions in real time. In my opinion, this is some of the best professional development out there. Teachers are the true masters of their grade level content. Why do we always feel like we have to pay somebody from out of state to deliver content training when someone in our backyard could do it in a more authentic way? Here is the key: you can't end your PLC meeting here. The majority of teachers will not transfer new learning to practice if you don't give them the opportunity to implement their new learning. The teachers were then split into small groups of 2-3 in which they planned a similar lesson to the one they observed that morning. Then they practiced teaching this lesson to a small group of students.

"Thank you for stretching me today, Mrs. Paschall. I will be honest with you; I probably wouldn't have ever tried this with my kids had you not made me work through the kinks today. I get so overwhelmed and intimidated with trying new things. This was the most powerful professional development I have ever had in my twenty years of teaching."

This was a typical response I repeatedly heard from teachers. Rather than always being so concerned with providing teachers the "what" in content training, let's slow down and let them also experience the "how."

For the remainder of the day, the PLC team planned additional lessons they would soon be teaching in their own classrooms. Each team met four times a year, at the beginning of each grading period. The reason for this was so that teachers could see an exemplary lesson that would set them up for success when they went back to their own classrooms. This PLC format created powerful communities across our school district. Teachers were finally networking with people beyond the four walls of their school, and academic equity was in full swing across our district, regardless of demographics or socio-economic status.

> Rather than always being so concerned with providing teachers the "what" in content training, let's slow down and let them also experience the "how."

How are you multiplying excellence in your school or school system? We often use the phrase "build teacher leader capacity." When we say this, let's be sure we aren't just focusing on growing our superstars into leaders. Culturize your school by creating a structure in which everyone is set up to successfully reach their personal excellence. Be sure that everyone is provided the necessary tools so that your school can successfully accomplish one of the greatest missions on the planet—leading every child to success.

If you really want to experience excellence, go out and multiply.

Multiply a relentless passion for kids.
Multiply exemplary instruction in classrooms.
Multiply support systems for all teachers.
Multiply excellence.

System of Excellence

If you're looking to begin a similar PLC format as described above, here are additional tips to help you get started:

1. Be strategic when forming your team. I can't stress this enough.
2. Begin by asking the PLC team what their greatest needs are. If you're working with a mix of teachers who are ranging in ability and needs, target the area that will most effectively promote academic equity.
3. Always meet with the teacher who will be observed ahead of time to develop a strategic plan for the day so you can best meet the needs of the teachers.
4. Before you bring the PLC team into the observed classroom, establish norms and expectations. In addition, provide them with specific "look fors" to take note of during the observation.

This will help to strengthen the conversation during the debrief. Sometimes it can be overwhelming to observe a high performing teacher. Giving them "look fors" will help to narrow the lens for them so they don't feel like they have to improve in so many areas at once.

5. When you pair the teachers up to teach a practice lesson, pair them up by mixed ability.

6. If there are instructional coaches at your school or district, involve them in this PLC process so they can follow up with coaching cycles to ensure follow through. This is critical.

7. Maintain ongoing support and follow-up with the PLC team throughout the nine weeks where they continue to provide resources and support one another.

8. At the end of each meeting, always, always, always ask for feedback from the team. What went well? What didn't go well? What were their biggest takeaways? How could the agenda be tweaked to make the day more beneficial in the future?

Learning to Fly

> "There is freedom waiting for you, on the breezes of the sky, and you ask, 'What if I fall?' Oh but my darling, what if you fly?"
>
> Erin Hanson

"Did the little birds fly away yet, Mommy?"

"Not yet baby, but they will soon!"

"But when?"

"When they're ready. Right now, they still need their momma to feed and take care of them, but soon, they will be strong enough to fly on their own!"

My three-year-old daughter was infatuated with the baby birds who nested in the eave of our front porch during the springtime. Every morning, she eagerly ran outside to see how they had changed and grown. She beamed with pride as she took note of their daily progress.

Witnessing the stages of a baby bird is one of life's greatest pleasures. There is something so gratifying about seeing a once completely dependent baby bird grow and gain the confidence to live independently in a few short weeks. In the beginning, the mother provides their every need, but slowly and instinctively, she begins to retract, knowing they are capable of accomplishing so much more. With nervous excitement we watch them build their strength and explore away from the safety of their home. As they perch on the rim of the nest, gathering their courage to lift off, we watch with bated breath as they exit the safety and security of the nest and flap their wings. "They did it!" we exclaim in our heads. "They learned to fly!" The birds fill themselves with pride as they circle the nest and expand their range and influence.

The mother bird nurtured her babies and stretched them to see beyond their limiting beliefs. The result? The baby birds took off and reached new, limitless heights they didn't know existed.

They learned to fly. They excelled. They were **empowered.**

"Empower" is another one of those words we loosely throw around in the world of education. How many times have you heard someone say, "I feel so empowered!" after listening to a motivational speech? Then a few days later, the person is back to their old habits, no longer holding on to that burst of energy and motivation. Why? Because they were never empowered in the first place. Self-empowerment is not something we feel. It is something we do. Our sense of empowerment is a reflection of the increased self-confidence that derives from our experience of knowing that what we are doing is making a difference.

If you want to create a culture of empowerment, you must first recognize that there are four different types of people in your building: hatchlings, nestlings, fledglings, and fliers.

1. **Hatchlings** are the baby birds who have just emerged from their egg—your brand-new teachers. I have seen many new teachers walk on eggshells each day because they don't know what their administrator is looking for or expecting. That's not fair. If you want to create a culture of excellence and partnership, allow your hatchlings to get to know you on a personal level by explaining your expectations and leadership style before the school year begins. Hatchlings need transparency and feedback.

Additionally, hatchlings need to be given a healthy balance of targeted support, as well as the freedom to try new things, fail, and try again. Hatchlings are developing their craft for the very first time. Nurture them as they embark on this journey and feed them with reassurance and confidence along the way. Before you know it, your hatchlings will be soaring.

2. A **nestling** is not yet ready to leave the nest. It does not have all of its feathers and can't stand up on its own. The nestlings in your school are the teachers who haven't yet advanced themselves professionally. Nestlings need two things to become empowered: honesty and self-confidence. Don't avoid the difficult conversations you may need to have with these teachers. It is the only way they will self-reflect and make a positive change. Otherwise, they will never leave the nest and learn to fly on their own. It really is kind to have an honest conversation. Avoiding them is the real tragedy because that is when we prevent the opportunity for growth and self-empowerment. Put proper supports in place to set them up for success as they make improvements, and flood them with encouragement along the way. Recognize and celebrate the things they are implementing that you want to see repeated.

If you have nestlings in your school who aren't intrinsically motivated to leave the nest and take flight, multiply excellence in your school by letting them go and replace them with a future flier.

3. A **fledgling** is a young bird that has all of its feathers and has left its nest on its own will, but its parents still feed and care for it. These teachers are diligent and consistent workers who are on the verge of flying, but they still lack the confidence to take flight. When fledglings lack self-confidence, they will never feel a sense of empowerment. For some fledglings, you're going to have to deconstruct the nest. When they become overly dependent, sometimes you have to retract support and remove their safety net. There is nothing wrong with pushing someone out of the nest. This is the only way they will learn to fly! Stretch teachers to see beyond their limiting beliefs by challenging them to find their own answer. Have an honest conversation with them. Assign them a peer mentor. Encourage them and build their capacity. Do whatever it takes to help them take flight. Productive perseverance produces grit, satisfaction, and empowerment. To struggle is good! Supply them with the ingredients, not the recipe.

Soon the fledglings will no longer need us, but it is because they have been empowered to fly. With the right push, they will make their own nest soon and thus multiply the excellence that we imparted in them.

4. Your **fliers** are self-empowered. They are your top performers who take control of their learning and growth, set goals, and confidently make positive choices. They are the ones who go above and beyond and deliver impeccable lessons day in and day out. They're soaring. The important thing to remember about your fliers is that they need encouragement and guidance too. Don't leave them out. You never want your fliers to stop flying. When people are overworked or underappreciated, self-empowerment can easily be replaced with burnout and resentment. Be the wind beneath their wings by challenging and nurturing them, as well as helping them to see the "next steps" they can take to multiply excellence in others.

It is important to understand that everyone is at different stages on their journey toward excellence. Recognize the stage each person is in and help them move through it by seeking the solution rather than fixating on the problem. Ignite an energy and enthusiasm within others to become stronger and more limitless than they ever imagined. Empowered teachers champion kids. Empowered teachers create a chain reaction of influence all around them. Empowered teachers multiply excellence.

Mama Don't Play

Be excellent.

Expect excellence from kids.

Expect excellence from staff members.

What's missing?

Parents. In order to culturize our schools and create the ultimate learning environment for kids, we must expect excellence from parents. They are an essential piece to the puzzle. But what do we do when parents don't know what excellence looks like? We build a relationship and enlighten them. That's what we do. Always keep the bar high.

Ms. Davis's Story

"Mrs. Paschall, I just wanted to let you know that Javon and Jamari missed two days again this week. That doesn't include the days they have been tardy. It appears that the mom's phone has been cut off again."

I received an update like this from their teacher every week. Javon and Jamari Davis were brothers in the second grade and they were chronically absent.

Both boys had failing grades.

Both boys didn't care about school.

Both boys needed a champion.

We had exhausted all of our efforts and resources in reaching the mother from the school, so it was time to take it to the house.

I asked the boys' classroom teacher and school counselor if they would be willing to go with me to Ms. Davis's house during the school day, and they immediately jumped at the opportunity.

"Hi Ms. Davis, my name is Mrs. Paschall. I'm one of the administrators from Javon and Jamari's school. We met this past summer when you enrolled your children, remember?"

Her eyes grew as wide as saucers.

"Oh hey Mrs. Paschall! Yes, I remember you."

"This is Mrs. Slater, our school counselor, and you already know the boys' teacher, Ms. Shields. It sure is great to see you again, Ms. Davis! How are you doing?"

I need to insert an important detail into this story. While greeting Ms. Davis, I gave her the warmest hug I knew how to give. When you do a surprise home visit, do everything within your control to let the parent know you are there to help and that you're both working on the same team to help their child. Body language, tone, and what you say with your eyes will either make or break this endeavor.

Immediately, Ms. Davis's demeanor softened. We made small talk for a moment, and then I cut to the chase.

"Ms. Davis, I want to explain to you why we've come by today but let me start by saying that we love your kids. We're here because we want what is best for them, and I know you do too."

"Yes ma'am, I sure do!"

"We are concerned about Javon and Jamari. They have missed so much school, and they don't appear to enjoy school on the days they are there. Are you noticing these same things?"

"Oh yes ma'am. I sure am. They won't get out of bed in the mornings. They straight up tell me they aren't going. It is a fight each day, and I am already struggling trying to keep track of their other two siblings who aren't in school yet. I don't know what I am going to do with them."

"Ms. Davis, both boys have failing grades. We so badly want to help them, but if they aren't at school, we can't reach them. I desperately need all of us working together to get them to school. I will do whatever it takes. If I need to come and help you pull them out of bed in the morning, I will. Bottom line, it is critical that we work more closely together. When I look at Javon and Jamari, I don't think about them in the present moment, I envision their future. Right now, Javon and Jamari are headed down a tough road; however, I have full confidence that we can rescue them, but only if we can get them to school."

Ms. Davis stared at me in silence for a solid five seconds. Then these words came out of her mouth:

"Wow. Thank you so much for caring, Mrs. Paschall. I don't know what else to say."

"We love your kids, Ms. Davis. I hope you know that."

"Oh yes ma'am. I sure do. I have never had a principal or teacher do anything like this. I dropped out of high school at 16 years old, and I wish someone had done this for me. Thank you."

We went on to make a plan with Ms. Davis about how we were going to work together to help her kids and scheduled for us to come back the following day for an additional home visit where we could discuss our concerns together with the boys.

"Listen boys. Y'all have got to start going to school every day. No more of this sleeping in and staying home. We are all working together on this, and Mrs. Paschall said if she has to come pull you out of bed herself, she will! She's serious! Trust me. Mama Paschall don't play!"

"Mama don't play." It cracked me up when Ms. Davis said this because this was the third time in my career that I had heard a parent say this about me. I may only be 5'4 (on a good day), but when I go to bat for a kid, I do it in a way that makes me feel 7 feet tall.

After entering their home, it became clear to us that Ms. Davis needed help in a much bigger way than just getting her kids out of bed in the morning. The kids' clothes and shoes didn't fit, the house was in terrible shape, and they didn't have enough food for five people to live on. As I sat there talking with the mother that day, I glanced over to see that our counselor had wrapped both toddlers up in her arms. They clung to her like they had known her their entire lives. The classroom teacher sat on the floor with the boys and did the most important thing—she formed a bond with them that she hadn't been able to form at school. It was a beautiful thing to witness. Over the next few weeks, our school counselor and social worker continued communicating with Ms. Davis so that they could provide assistance with parenting skills, food needs, and other vital resources, including a prepaid phone so that the mother could consistently reach out to the social worker for parenting help. The boys' teacher became much more devoted as well by visiting their home to help the boys with their schoolwork. While my initial persistence may have been the catalyst to discovering their needs, it was the investment from everyone else that made the true difference. They were the true champions who created a plot twist for this family.

Expect excellence from parents, no ifs, ands, or buts about it. Always expect excellence, but when you do it, make sure you set them up for success and support them along the way. Parents are typically raising their children in the best—or only—way they know how.

Humble yourself.
Build a relationship.
Be a catalyst.
And be their champion.

System of Excellence

As educators, sometimes it is hard for us to fathom why some parents would choose to raise their child in a certain way.

Maybe a kid comes to school every day looking like he has just rolled out of bed.

Maybe dad is more concerned about his social life than spending time with his child.

Maybe the grandparents are too exhausted to be raising yet another grandchild and never make sure that homework gets completed.

Maybe the kid stays home alone in the evenings because mom is working two jobs to make ends meet.

Maybe dad devotes too much time to work rather than cherishing quality family time.

Maybe mom is a drug addict.

From the outside looking in, it's easy to see the better choices parents could be making or how much "better off" a child could be under different circumstances. Let's be careful with that mentality. Parents are typically raising their child in the best or only way they know how. Being poor doesn't make you a bad parent, no more than being rich makes you a good one. Rich or poor, parents are usually raising their own kids as they were raised. They want the best for their children and for the most part give them the best they know. The challenge in schools is to help parents become better at being parents. As educators, we need to be ready to help them if and when it is within our realm of control.

1. Humble yourself

As a staff, have a conversation about your students' parents. What are some positives that you see? Make a list of the concerns that you have. Now for the hard part: Try to understand the parents' perspective by looking through their lens. Why do you think they have chosen this pathway?

Humble yourself. When we replace criticism with compassion, we open our own window of receptivity to approach the situation with honesty, sincerity, and gentleness. Don't fool yourself into thinking parents don't sense the difference.

2. Build a relationship.

How can you work to build a stronger relationship with all parents? The stronger the school-to-home connection is, the more likely it will be that you help all students succeed.

The teacher/parent connection must be:

Genuine. Create a bond that is natural, not forced. Show a sincere interest in getting to know more about them. Relationships with parents won't ever be formed through texting apps such as Remind or DOJO. While these are great platforms for providing quick communication, it is no place to form a bond. Texting apps are a great place to miscommunicate your feelings, as well as misconceive what someone else meant.

Positive in nature - even during negative times. When you know parents are struggling, ask, "How are you doing?" and "How can we help?"

Honest. Sometimes, parents need to hear the truth. When the relationship is there, this opens the door to have those necessary, hard conversations. Their window of receptivity will be wide open when they feel confident that you are working with, rather than against, them.

3. Be a catalyst and be their champion!

Now that you've made a list as a faculty about the concerns you have regarding parenting skills, what are you going to do about it? It's important to put a proactive structure in place so that you can find a way to help them.

If parents are devoting too much time to their work or social life rather than cherishing quality family time, **plan a family night.**

If you have students who are home alone in the evenings because their parents are working two jobs to make ends meet, **develop an after school and/or summer program.**

When you have parents who are struggling to meet their child's physiological needs, **are teachers aware of the available resources and organizations in the community that can be of help to these families?** So many classroom teachers fork out their own money to help their poorest students. I've seen it happen time and time again. While this is a wonderful thing, making constant purchases can lead to stress within their own families, as well as emotional burnout when they try to take these things on themselves. It is critical that teachers are made aware of organizations that can help (e.g., food banks, clothing closets, safe houses, employment agencies, church supports, Federal Program supports, etc.). Have your school counselor create a one-page document that lists all of the community resources and create a QR code so this is easily accessible to everyone.

Parents don't need schools to be their Santa Claus. They need schools to provide guidance and support. When you see an area in which parents are lacking necessary skills, put a targeted support system in place within your school.

If you want to champion your students, champion their parents too. Replace criticism with compassion and help them break the cycle of repeating what they know. Help them see a better way and fill themselves with dignity. Help parents multiply excellence!

Below are three culture building ideas that schools can put into practice to build a culture of excellence. When practices such as these are in place, the leadership capacity in your school will multiply.

Culture Builders

1. Get on the Bus! - Before we expect excellence from others, we must first be excellent ourselves. The level of excellence a school will reach stems from effective leadership. Building relationships with students should be a key focus, and the school bus is one of the best places to make that happen. Set the example by being a bus rider. Commit to riding the bus one time every week. When you do this, invite teachers to join along with you. This could even become a part of #FaceLiftFridays where you surprise the kids every Friday morning by riding a bus. Leadership starts from the top. Your example will create a chain reaction in championing for kids at a new level.

2. Flip Your Faculty Meetings - When we lead faculty meetings of a "sit and get" format, we need to reflect on the example we are setting. Faculty meetings like these model anti-engagement, anti-best teaching practices, and anti-community building—the opposite of everything we ask teachers to do on a daily basis. Flip your faculty meetings so that you can use this coveted time to grow as a staff. Community building isn't something we should only do the week before school starts. A culturized school is focused on building a community all year long. If your list of faculty meeting notes can be stated in an email, don't discuss it in your faculty meetings. Cherish the limited time you have with your colleagues each month by taking opportunities to build relationships and leadership capacity.

Utilize this time to enjoy being around one another, discuss how you can fix the broken windows in your school, and work toward academic excellence. Another idea is that you can flip your faculty meetings by utilizing this time to do a book study. This is a great way to build on the common focus in your school, as well as allow teachers the opportunity to reflect and grow in their teaching practices in real time. Additionally, this is the ideal time and place to allow teachers to get their feet wet with leading their peers. Model excellence by flipping your faculty meetings.

3. Teacher-Led Learning Walks - Once you have begun implementing the Cycle of Academic Excellence as described in this chapter, begin making a shift which allows teachers to begin leading the learning walk process. It is important to keep in mind that you don't want to make this shift too quickly. If the Cycle of Academic Excellence is new for your school, your administrative team may want to lead the learning walks the entire first year. The following year, you could slowly begin retracting your lead role in the process while gradually handing the reins over to the teachers. Administrators should never be the only instructional leaders in the building. A culture of academic excellence stems from intrinsically-motivated and self-empowered teachers as instructional leaders

Reflection Questions

1. Share about a time someone challenged you to grow in a certain area. How did you respond? Was your window of vulnerability open and ready to recognize areas of needed improvement, or did you resist the feedback?

2. Describe a way you stay innovative in improving your craft so you continuously soar above the status quo?

3. Name a current broken window in your classroom/school/district's academic focus. What is a strength? In reference to the Cycle of Academic Excellence Chart, how are you all moving through each step of this cycle?

4. How will you multiply excellence within yourself? In your school? Among your students' families?

CHAPTER 4

Core Principle 3: Carry the Banner

Shout from the Rooftop

When I was a first-grade teacher, one of my students came prancing into my classroom one morning with a huge "7" taped to the front of her shirt.

"Good morning, Olivia! Tell me about..."

"MY BIRTHDAY IS IN 7 DAYS! MY BIRTHDAY IS IN 7 DAYS!"

"It is? Well how exciting! Do you have big plans for your birthday?"

"Uh huh. It's going to be a unicorn party. With unicorn cupcakes. And unicorn plates. And I get to dress up like a unicorn!"

"Oh, how fun! I can't wait for that day to get here. I know you're going to have so much fun."

The next day, Olivia came strolling into my classroom, this time with a giant "6" taped to her shirt.

"Good morn..."

"MY BIRTHDAY IS IN 6 DAYS! MY BIRTHDAY IS IN 6 DAYS!"

Olivia went on to ecstatically share more details about her birthday. You couldn't help but laugh and smile at how excited this little girl was. Her joy was so contagious that she had the teachers sharing about it at the lunch table. Every day after that, Olivia burst into my classroom with the updated final countdown on her shirt. When the big day finally arrived, she came waltzing into school wearing a unicorn outfit, topped with a unicorn headband. And you better believe her mom followed her inside with those unicorn plates and cupcakes!

Some of you may remember the episode from the show *Friends* when Monica and Chandler got engaged, and Monica blissfully and unashamedly shouted, "I'm engaged, I'm engaged!" from the rooftop? Olivia's excitement level easily equated to this. There is no better comparison. Olivia loudly and proudly carried the banner for her upcoming birthday party.

We could all learn some important lessons about leadership from Olivia:

1. She had a clear vision.
2. She was passionate.
3. She explicitly communicated her vision and passion with others.

By the time Olivia's big day finally arrived, she wasn't the only one who was excited her birthday was finally here. We all were, kids and teachers included! Why? Because her excitement was infectious. All week long, she shouted from the rooftop, and her excitement had made everyone else excited.

How does your level of communication, zeal, and positivity for your school or school system measure up with Olivia's? Do the people around you know where your school stands regarding your convictions of what's best for kids? Or do others have to make up their own assumptions about where your school stands because you haven't clearly expressed it?

Take a moment to reread those last three sentences. It's important to note that all three questions ask about 'your school's banner', not *your* banner. A culturized school doesn't have multiple banners.

One school. One vision. One banner.

How you carry the banner for your school will do one of two things: it will either contribute toward driving your school's culture backward or forward. Throughout this chapter, I hope that you gain a deeper understanding of the importance in carrying the banner for your school, as well as how to go about tackling this. While we may never wear a shirt with our school's vision taped to the front, our convictions and core beliefs should be as obvious as Olivia's.

No one should ever have to guess what your school's banner says. Be loud. Be proud. And shout your beliefs about kids from the rooftop.

Mindset Matters

It's a very common phenomenon to get so caught up in the obligations of everyday life—work, relationships, kids, errands, social commitments, family gatherings—that we end up making very little time for ourselves, if any at all.

This was my reality a few years ago. I was juggling the hats of teacher, grad school student, wife, new mom, housekeeper, friend, daughter—the list goes on. My mornings were far from leisurely as I took a quick shower, threw on a little makeup, and scarfed down my breakfast. My school day teaching 9-year-olds flew by in a flurry, and my evenings were equally rushed as I got home in just enough time to slap dinner together. Get Avery to bed, brush teeth, hit the pillow, wake up, repeat. I was trying to be all things to all people—everyone except for myself, that is. I was physically and mentally exhausted, and my cup was empty.

I'll never forget driving home one Monday afternoon after a long and hard day of work, with a mind full of negative thoughts. I was already counting down the days to the weekend, wanting to speed up the precious time I had left with my students. On top of that, I didn't look forward to going home to prepare dinner and take care of my family. How unfair that was to them. They hadn't done anything wrong. The problem was inside me. Family is supposed to be our joyful safe haven, but my mind was too exhausted to appreciate the blessings that were in front of me. I wish I could tell you that I immediately recognized the root cause of my problem, but I didn't. I struggled through that entire semester. My biggest issue? I had surrendered control of my attitude.

Mindset matters!

That summer, I reflected on my poor attitude and what I needed to do to work on *me*. I began forcing myself to take time *for* myself by adding exercise into my daily routine. It's amazing what thirty minutes of self-care can do for your mindset. Without self-care, doubt, resentment, and negativity begin to creep in. I had no idea how badly I needed this devoted time until I learned what it was like to go without it.

In addition, I began compartmentalizing my anxieties and stresses by asking myself one simple question: Is it inside or outside my realm of control? I'm a work in progress at trying to train my brain to think in quadrants like in the image on the following page. First, decide the level of importance this stressor has in your life. Then decide what you're going to do about it.

Mindset Management Quadrant

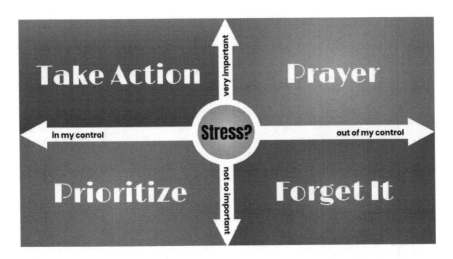

Do I still battle with my attitude some days? Of course! But now I know what is necessary to give myself a needed reset. Life is full of ups and downs, and these ups and downs come in different shapes and sizes for everyone.

Maybe you're caring for a sick loved one.

Maybe you're facing financial struggles.

Maybe you're in a new role at school this year and feel as if you're drowning.

Maybe you're living in a broken home.

Regardless of what you're facing, your battle is hard simply because it is the hardest thing you are going through at this time in your life. Don't diminish that. Trying to shove our battles to the side is one of the worst things we can do. The trick is to take action on what is within your power and find the grit inside you to let go of what you cannot change.

While we may not have any power over the storms that come our way, we always have control over two things: our attitude and our effort.

We can't let things that are beyond our control get in the way of being our best for kids, **ever**. My students and coworkers relied on me to carry the banner, but without my mindset in the right place, I would never do this to the fullest. Kids didn't sign up for a distracted, negative teacher. Give your students the best of you, not what's left of you. Kids must know that hail or high water, we are

> Kids didn't sign up for a distracted, negative teacher. Give your students the best of you, not what's left of you.

going to continue moving forward. Each year, each month, each day, each hour, minute, and second are too valuable to waste. Once gone, that learning opportunity is lost forever. Don't carry these stressors with you into your classroom. Whatever is going on outside of your classroom will have to wait. We can't let it ruin our precious time with our students. They need us, and we must be mentally prepared to bring it every single day.

Are you feeling bogged down with life's cumulative stresses? Are these stressors stealing the joys of what you get to do each day? Standing around and complaining about it will get you nowhere. Take action! Don't let your mind bully the joy of being a teacher. It's not about getting your life together or hoping for perfection. It's about attitude and effort. Mindset matters! Even when the world is on fire, or we're suddenly trudging through a global pandemic, kids need us to bring our best every single day. When you are in control of your mindset, that is when you will begin to carry the banner. That is when transformation will begin to take place. That's when change will occur. That is when you multiply excellence.

Love Your School

"This is my mission, to sow into these tender hearts while they are still sponges, before the ground gets too hard. Now that God has planted me here to work, I'm going to do what they have me to do—clean this building! But I'm not going to blow my opportunity to make a greater difference!" (Good, 2016)

His name was Jerome Lewis. Jerome was a custodian at an elementary school in Birmingham, Alabama.

Hardworking. Sincere. Encouraging. Jubilant. Zealous. Humble.

These are just a few words one might have used to describe him.

He loved his school and all of the people who filled it. Many days, he showed up to work at least an hour and a half early so that he could mentally prepare his mind for the school day. If you saw him in the hallway and asked how he was doing, his response would always be, "Blessed and grateful," even on his worst days.

Jerome Lewis radiated constant joy.

"It's exciting. I love coming to work! This is a home. This place is like family. When one part hurts, all hurts. When one part rejoices, all rejoices. That is why I am here." (Good, 2016)

Jerome's infectious personality and love for his school was captivating. It was a common occurrence that former students and parents would come back to the school just to see him. He had the lowest paying job in the school, but everyone who knew him would effortlessly admit that he carried the greatest influence. The impact he made in the community stretched far beyond the hallways.

"A lot of people, when they think about janitors, think they don't make a big difference," one student said. "They think NBA players or basketball players are the difference makers. But a janitor like Mr. Jerome does a lot. Mr. Jerome has changed our entire community." (Good, 2016)

Jerome was intentional about learning every kid's name in the school. "I know I'm just a custodian, but I make myself friendly." Jerome remarked. "When you get on a first name basis with them, it helps them to give in to you, talk to you, and be more free." He gave his all every single day. His job as a janitor wasn't just a job, it was his purpose. This was his calling. And the students adored him for it.

"I know it may sound obsolete to you, but it's true what I'm saying. I draw strength from being around these kids. I glean strength from being around these kids. It keeps me focused. Whether it's fair weather or a storm, I want them to still see me exemplify the same smile as God." (Good, 2016) His prayer was that God let his radiance and countenance continue to shine, in spite of any darkness or affliction.

Jerome loved his school, and his mission to sow into young and tender hearts created a ripple effect in the entire community. It would be impossible to count the number of seeds he sowed. How does your passion for your school compare to Jerome's? Do you radiate positivity? Does your mission align with Jerome's? If your school's community only knew about your school based on how you present yourself, what would its reputation be?

Carrying the banner for your school begins with loving your school, plain and simple. Do you exude a positive energy that shows you want to be there each day? We are in the kid business. Serving as an educator should not be viewed as work; it's a calling.

I used to have a bad habit of saying things like, "I have to get these papers graded," or "I have to teach a math lesson in a first-grade classroom today," unaware of how negative I sounded. One of my coworkers began correcting me every time he noticed it by saying, "You don't *have* to, you *get* to!" How right he was. Language matters. Working with kids is a "get to" opportunity. Carry the banner for your school by choosing a "get to" mentality. Speak with a language that makes others want to be part of what you get to do each day.

Nobody wants to work with a negative or unhappy person. When you talk about your school, do you put it in a positive light? What stories do you tell on the weekends while you sit at your child's ballgame? What do you say about your coworkers? Do you talk about your school at all? What you say about your school and the people who fill it will either carry or trample the banner. There is no in between. You are the beginning of your school's reputation.

Be like Jerome Lewis. Choose positivity so that you can sow into as many tender hearts as possible before the ground gets too hard. Love your school and the people who fill it. Don't allow negativity to blow your opportunity to make a greater difference.

Love multiplies. Love your job. Love the people. Love your school.

> What you say about your school and the people who fill it will either carry or trample the banner. There is no in between. You are the beginning of your school's reputation.

Carry the Banner Together

Each year, my hometown participates in a *Relay for Life* event to support our local cancer patients. The event is twelve hours in length, and like any typical *Relay for Life* event, each team is asked to have a member on the track at all times to signify that cancer never sleeps. Cancer patients don't stop for a rest because they are tired, and for this one night, no one else does either. The walk begins at 8:00 p.m. and ends the following morning at 8:00 a.m.

Several years ago, a middle-aged man participated in the event to honor his spouse. He decided to walk all night long without taking any breaks. In addition, he held a large flag high in the air with nothing supporting him to carry the flag except his own physical strength.

12 hours of walking.
12 hours holding a flag high in the air.
12 hours without a break.

He never complained. When others offered to take his spot, he kindly declined and continued to push through it. He relentlessly carried the banner for something he loved and stood for. This man wowed the entire crowd that night. People on the sidelines cheered and screamed for him as he rounded every corner. When he crossed the finish line, tears of pride and exhaustion streamed down his face. It was an emotional moment for every person who witnessed it.

There are two parts to this story that stand out to me:

1. He was unequivocally devoted to loving and supporting what he stood for.
2. He had a support system on the sidelines who not only cheered him on but were also ready to carry his flag for him if he grew weak.

He no longer had to worry about carrying the flag alone. A multitude of people were invested in making sure the flag continued to fly, no matter what. As educators, we don't carry our own individual banners. We carry one banner together.

One school. One vision. One banner.

Carrying the banner for your school begins with loving your school, but the reality is that we are all human, and we are going to have weak moments where the banner becomes too heavy to carry alone. I've said it before, and I'll say it again. Teaching is arguably the hardest job on the planet. When your coworkers begin to feel weak, do you help them carry the banner, or do you allow them to put the banner to rest?

Do you enable or empower others?

The desire to help others when they fall weak is a noble, instinctive reaction by the human race. We naturally want to help our friends solve the problems life throws at them. The issue, however, arises when we offer help that perpetuates, rather than solves, the problem. When you enable a coworker's problems, you take away all motivation for the person to take responsibility for his or her own actions. Without that motivation, there is no desire for the person to change. You're only allowing them to dig a deeper hole.

A teacher who allows a student to not complete his classwork because of his wrecked homelife is enabling irresponsibility.

The teacher who makes excuses for her underperforming coworker enables the status quo mentality.

The principal who won't have that honest conversation enables a teacher to be content with low data year after year.

While educators should be understanding of a student's homelife, educators must always maintain a standard of excellence by not allowing excuses and situations to derail the student's potential.

As teachers, when we see that our coworker is underperforming, don't coddle them by allowing excuses to creep in. Deflect their excuses and reply with positive words and energy that refocuses your coworker. We must counteract their weakness and restore them. Bring your coworker back to the banner.

Do you know what your school's banner says? Are you willing to carry it? When a co-worker or staff member is growing weak or off-course are you willing to encourage and empower them? Carry the banner together and you can move the entire school forward.

Know Your Banner

One of the most iconic artifacts in the world is the American Flag. Each day, people all over the country hang the flag with awe and respect. Many people take comfort in seeing it, knowing that it symbolizes the heart and soul of what our country stands for: liberty. After the tragedy of 9/11, our flag waved among the rubble of the Twin Towers to symbolize our nation's unconquerable spirit. The renowned photo taken at Iwo Jima became famous because it represented the resilience of our U.S. military during World War II. Seeing our waving flag at parades and major sporting events makes many Americans beam with pride. We wear it on our shirts, lapel jackets, and cars because it fills us with a sense of purpose and belonging. In times of happiness, sorrow, or uncertainty, the American Flag remains our stronghold and reminds us that regardless of any circumstance, we are bound together as one union of people. The American Flag is the banner of America.

One nation. One heart. One flag.

Consider your school's banner. What does it signify? Do you know? More importantly, does your staff know? If our community, our students, and especially our teachers in the building don't know what is on the banner, it might as well be folded up in the closet. Oftentimes, I am afraid we get so wrapped up in the process of writing an official vision and mission statement that it causes us to forget the true purpose of its existence: to represent the heart and soul of everything we stand for in education. While creating something like this is critical, let's be careful not to let it become an empty statement that we don't find ourselves connecting with on a daily basis. A school's banner should be the very heart of what the school is all about.

One school. One vision. One banner.

What's written on your banner doesn't have to be formal, nor does it have to be perfectly articulated. Don't let overused jargon interfere with the real purpose of what you're trying to do here. Your school's banner should be a steadfast reminder that your purpose in education is greater than any challenge that comes your way. Scripting your banner will not only define expectations of what it looks like to love the school you are a part of, but it will also open the door of accountability among coworkers when one's mindset begins to waver. If you've found yourself struggling with what to say to a coworker who has lost their way, chances are high that your school's banner hasn't been clearly articulated. A school's banner should be written in a way that provides clear direction, as well as opportunity for self-reflection when we need to get our mindsets in check.

Below is a sample of what a *Banner of Excellence* might say:

1. Connection before content
2. Define expectations
3. Love your students, coworkers, and job relentlessly
4. Be a sponge with a growth mindset
5. Expect excellence from **all** kids, regardless of circumstances
6. Give yourself and others grace
7. Strive for excellence

Write the banner together. Memorize it. Expect it. Model it. Live it. Believing in positive thoughts is the single greatest catalyst toward success. Allow your school's banner to become the mantra that helps to bust through subconscious barriers which exist in a school. This is when you will evoke a true positive change. This is when you will carry the banner together. This is when you will multiply excellence.

System of Excellence

Before you begin writing a vision and mission statement, it's important to know what's on your banner. If you don't, chances are high that the mission and vision statements will be empty words. How can you know where you're going if you don't know what's on your banner to begin with? A school's banner should signify the heart and soul of everything you are about. Think of it through the lens of non-negotiables. What will everyone relentlessly commit to doing for the betterment of kids each day? Non-negotiables are black and white, and they provide a clear, unified focus. These will help you to know what to collectively expect from one another.

Below is an idea of how your staff could collaborate to script the banner for your school.

Begin by strategically dividing your staff into groups of 4-5. Mix up the grade levels and personality types, and ask them to discuss these simple questions:

1. What do we do?
2. Why do we do it?

This will get the conversation flowing among the groups. It is important that you get their wheels spinning about their true purpose. Then follow up with this critical question:

In order to multiply excellence in every child, what non-negotiable commitments must we abide by as a staff?

Have each group create a list of 5-7 non-negotiables. Then allow the teams to travel to each group so they can see one another's ideas. Ask them to use a different colored marker to add questions or make comments. After this process has been completed, allow the groups to travel back to their original lists to jot down additional notes if anyone asked a clarifying question.

On a different day, allow a team of people to categorize everyone's responses. Some ideas will be repeated. Some ideas will be similar. Use these lists to nail down what the most important non-negotiables were among the faculty. Create a list to present back to the faculty. Let them have input on things that need to be reworded, cut out, or added.

Once the list is final, let the words on the banner become ingrained inside of you by always coming back to the banner. When you meet together, project it for everyone to see and ask these questions:

How are we doing?

What is an area of strength?

How can we be better?

Make time to periodically self-reflect and discuss areas of needed improvement to continuously monitor their mindset. Encourage and hold one another accountable by frequently going back to the banner. This banner should be the heart of what you are all about. Don't allow it to become empty, forgotten words. Memorize it. Expect it. Model it. And live it.

Wave Your Banner with Pride

When I stepped into an administrative role at Cedar Hill Elementary, I quickly realized that it was one of the best kept secrets in the state of Alabama. The administration team was strong, and the teachers and students were incredible. To top it all off, the surrounding community was equally devoted to the kids in our school. When I was selected to join the Cedar Hill family I felt as if I had struck gold getting to be part of such a wonderful team.

Great things were happening every day. Teachers were delivering rich and engaging lessons. The custodians exuded a positive energy that was contagious. The receptionist created a wonderful first impression for the school. The entire faculty and staff were carrying the banner, but we needed to find a way to wave it high enough for others to see. Don't let the magic you're creating each day be confined to the four walls of your school.

Realizing we had so many excellent things to share, our staff made a schoolwide goal to begin telling our story in real time, all year long. We were determined to put Cedar Hill on the map. The following school year, the staff worked tirelessly to showcase the great things that were happening each day. Below are four action steps we took that made a big difference in promoting positivity for our school:

1. Parent Volunteers

Not including parents in the day-to-day activities of your school opens the door to too much negative imagination in the minds of parents. Fear, uncertainty, feeling you have something to hide, and negativity creeps in when parents do not know what is going on inside the school walls. Invite parents into your school and classrooms. Let them help you manage learning stations, prepare materials for upcoming lessons, decorate bulletin boards—anything that allows them to become a part of the school community. Parents are entrusting you with their most prized possessions five days a week. Be intentional about making them feel confident and excited about where they are sending their children each day.

2. Partner with Local Businesses

Community members can serve a critical role in moving your school forward. Let them become part of shaping kids' futures. One way we did this was by partnering with one of our local banks to create a program called "School Bank." One morning a month, bank employees arrive at Cedar Hill before school to allow kids to deposit money into a savings account. Kids eagerly line up to deposit their money, ranging from twenty-five cents to one hundred dollars. The bank employees take the time to engage in conversation with each child who makes a deposit. By the end of the year, they knew almost every one of the kids' names. The benefits were twofold. Not only did we support a local business, but the bank employees also had the opportunity to see how we begin every school day at Cedar Hill. As soon as our kids arrive, we are standing there ready to greet them with loud music and hugs. Every morning at Cedar Hill is special and exciting, and the bank employees love to be part of it once a month. Since forming this partnership, First National Bank has made multiple financial donations to our school. Why? Because they believe in our banner. When community members are equally invested in what you're doing, the sky's the limit for your school.

3. Invite Outsiders

You never know who or what will multiply your school's excellence. An administrator once made a post on social media inviting senior citizens from the community to attend Grandparents Day Lunch so they could sit with students whose grandparents could not attend. One couple in their late 80's had so much fun they returned the next day to ask what they could do to regularly be at the school. The couple wanted a reason to become part of what they were doing each day. The administrator noticed the previous week that the school's secretary was having to spend time after school to do all that needed to be done to stock and sort the food pantry for the weekend backpack program. The administrator asked the secretary if she would accept quality help if he could find it. "Gladly," she quickly replied with a smile. So he asked the senior couple if they would be willing to help. Since that day, they have not missed a week of stocking the school's food pantry in over five years. Not only do they come each week, but they also contact the churches on the pantry's needs and talk to people and groups about donations. That simple post on social media has resulted in partners that are continuing to carry the banner.

4. Wave Your Banner on Social Media

How you present your school is how people will view it. What are you showcasing? Good leaders don't just utilize social media to circulate information. They use it to prick the public mind with yearning and hope. Good leaders leave them craving more. Social media is one of the most impactful ways to promote positivity for your school. Allow it to become your story book for each and every school day. Not only does it showcase your school, but it also makes teachers feel good about their impact. This is a great way to validate teachers for the magic they are creating. Teachers work hard day in and day out, and they deserve that reassurance from a simple acknowledgment via a post of the great things they are doing. It is critical that administrators model this so that teachers will do the same for their colleagues and students. Additionally, it is encouraging to the community to see what is happening, even to people who don't have kids in school.

Negative energy will quickly move a school culture backward, but no energy leaves your school in a highly vulnerable state because it means your school's banner is at rest. When you keep the day-to-day magic contained, you can't multiply excellence. No energy leads to negative energy. Don't fall prey to this. Wave your banner by intentionally promoting positivity. Don't be afraid to tell your school's story. This isn't arrogant; this is showing school pride. Social media shouldn't be used with the intent of impressing others, but rather to impact others. Tell it in a way that makes others want to be a part of it.

Let Others Carry the Banner for You

Mr. Jackson's Story

An aspiring administrator anxiously prepared to interview for a principalship at a once-proud school that had become worn and let go: Fountain Elementary School. The bank account had suffered a similar fate, leaving the balance near zero. If James Jackson were selected, he would have a major rehabilitation project on his hands with very little in the way of financial resources.

It was the start of an already scorching summer. It was interview day and Jackson arrived on the campus an hour early. He had spent the day driving around the town meeting community members. Most of the people had little positive remarks to make about the school, and those who did only spoke of yesteryears. The campus was littered with trash. The knee-high grass made walking around the buildings an adventure. The buildings all had chipped paint and were surrounded by overgrown shrubs and vines. Two mismatched shoes adorned the fieldhouse roof.

Jackson's stomach was riddled with nerves from the impending interview, but equally uneasy with what he had seen and heard.

As the interview started it quickly became apparent that the interview committee members loved their school and wanted a champion. The interview went very well as they were impressed that Jackson had learned about their community, as well as the interior and exterior of their school.

When the superintendent handed him the keys, he asked, "What are you going to do first?" James Jackson grinned and said, "I am getting those shoes off the roof!" Jackson left his office and quickly drove home to change clothes and gather a ladder, tools, and weed trimmer. He hit the ground running because so much needed to be done. On the first day, Jackson collected ten large bags of trash just so he could cut the grass. Traffic slowed as they passed by the school, but no one stopped.

Day two was more of the same. He trimmed bushes and trees and cleaned out gutters. Jackson was disgusted to realize that the trash-free campus he left the day before again had multiple bags of rubbish to be picked up. Near the conclusion of the second day, an elderly man stopped by to introduce himself. "My name is Jim Miller. You must be new here." Jim asked if he was planning to work the rest of the week. "Yes sir. This is the greatest school in the district, and I have to get it ready because the teachers and students will be coming back in August." Jim laughed as he walked away.

Day three began with trash pickup. "How can there possibly be so much trash on this campus," he thought to himself. Today's priority was to pressure wash the buildings to see what was below the grit and grime. Busy with his task he had not seen Jim arrive. Jim and his grandson, Tony, had brought their pressure washer and were working on the opposite side of the building. Tony was a 7th grade student at the school, quiet but extremely hard working. Jim, Tony, and Mr. Jackson ate a monster cheeseburger at the local cafe to celebrate their hard work. While they were there, Jim introduced Jackson to everyone in the building. "What do you have planned tomorrow, Mr. Jackson?" Jim asked as they exited the cafe. "I'm going to scrape paint off, sand, and hopefully start to paint some exterior walls." Jim smiled and said, "What color, boss?" "White. I want the building to look as bright and clean as possible."

As Jackson drove to the school for day four, he giggled to himself, wondering if ol' Jim would be climbing a ladder to scrape, sand, and paint the eaves and cornices of the brick school that day. Mr. Jackson stopped by the hardware store on the way, so he arrived later than usual. When he got there, a crew of twenty-five men were busy scraping and sanding. When Mr. Jackson introduced himself to all of them, the man in charge explained that after his boss had met Jackson in the cafe the previous day, he told his crew, "You all are to paint the school today. And paint it white because we have the best school in the district, and we need to get it ready for the teachers and students." James Jackson learned a lot about how to paint from those professionals that day. The painters learned about his passion and vision for the students and their school. Most of them had attended the school as students, and many of them currently had children in the school. As Jackson was packing up to leave, another work truck pulled up. It was the Mayor. "Well hey there, sir. I'm here to meet Tony's hero. Are you Mr. Jackson?" Tony was friends with his son and had spent the night at the Mayor's home the previous night. The Mayor laughed as he said, "That boy thinks you hung the moon. Tony is so excited about coming to our 'new' school."

Over the next few weeks, different community members continued to show up to get the work done. You never knew who would show up or when they would arrive. All of the labor was free, and every bit of effort stemmed from the community's passion and commitment to Fountain Elementary School

Come August, the students and staff began their school year in a "new" school. The community, teachers, and students were exploding with excitement. Students who had moved to neighboring schools enrolled back in Fountain Elementary School. Alumni wanted to tour the school and purchase school swag. Jim and the Mayor stopped by as Mr. Jackson was preparing for a football game. Jackson thanked them for all they had done to help the school. Jim and the Mayor both beamed with pride and excitement. Jim heartedly patted Mr. Jackson on the back and said, "Our community needed you!" Jackson thanked and retorted, "The community has done all of it. You guys are amazing!" Jim replied, "We were lacking someone who would work to make our school the best. We all want to be part of that."

If Jackson had not changed the culture by no longer accepting shoes on the roof and trash in the yard, then the community would not have jumped in to help. The community loved their school and were willing to do what it took to make it the best. Jackson's job was to lead and gain momentum. By carrying the banner for his school, not making excuses, or demanding money or help, others willingly and wholeheartedly jumped in. As a result, Mr. Jackson was able to step aside so that he could focus on the main thing: the students and the classrooms of their "new" school.

What are parents and the community saying about your school? Do you give them a reason to want to talk about it? You see, it can't just be administrators and faculty members carrying the banner. It is about what others are saying. When people feel like they are a part of the school community, they will begin to carry the banner for you. Be a James Jackson. Create the experiences and treat people in a way that results in them carrying the banner and wanting more. When this happens, that is when you know you have culturized your school. That is when you will multiply excellence.

Be an Olivia

"Good morning, Olivia! We're two days away from your birthday! I'm so..."

133

Before I could finish my sentence, Olivia zipped past me, pranced straight into our classroom, and began placing something on each kids' desk. Out of curiosity, I walked up to get a closer look of what it might be. You guessed it. Unicorn themed invitations for her class party. Each invitation was sealed in an envelope, and each envelope contained a sheet of unicorn stickers, you know, in case some of the kids didn't have any unicorn gear to wear on the big day.

"Hey Shelly! I have your invitation for my party!"

"Thanks, Olivia! I am so excited! My mom is buying me a unicorn shirt today to wear to school on your birthday!"

I listened to that conversation in amazement that day. Never had I seen a group of kids get so excited over a class birthday party. When the big day finally arrived, not one, not two, but three girls showed up in a unicorn shirt! And the ones who didn't have a special shirt decorated their arms and faces with their unicorn stickers.

Olivia did everything right in carrying the banner for her birthday party. In every way, she carried it to the fullest! To summarize and wrap up this chapter, I want to highlight some important lessons we can learn from Olivia as we work to carry the banner in our own schools:

Mindset Matters

Olivia's mindset was in the right place from day one. Once she had developed a clear vision, she took action of what was in her control and seamlessly executed her plan. Olivia didn't allow any outside stressors (like completing her classwork) to get in the way of preparing for her party. She maintained control of her mindset and mentally prepared herself to stay the course every single day.

Reflect on the *Mindset Management Quadrant* near the beginning of this chapter. What is an area in which you need to pull yourself together and prioritize to maximize your impact as an educator?

Love Your School

Olivia loved her birthday. Her family knew it. Her friends knew it. Her teachers knew it. I'm pretty sure the birds outside even knew it! In just one week's time, she created a ripple effect within our school. Olivia's love for her birthday made others want to be a part of it.

If your school's community only knew about your school based on how you present yourself, what would its reputation be?

When you're working in the kid business, you must either love what you do, or not do it at all. This is absolute. There is no grey area when we're shaping future generations. Love what you do, and let your excitement be written all over your face.

Carry the Banner Together

Everyone in our class carried the same banner on Olivia's birthday, even down to our matching unicorn garb and stickers. Each person was equally invested in ensuring that this birthday party went off without a hitch.

Are you carrying the same banner as your coworkers? When your coworkers begin to feel weak, do you help them carry the banner, or do you allow them to put the banner to rest?

One school. One vision. One banner.

When your coworkers grow weary or discouraged, empower rather than enable them. Whatever you do, don't ever let the banner stop waving.

Know Your Banner

Olivia's birthday banner was written in a way that provided clear direction. She had a clear vision, she was passionate, and she explicitly communicated her vision and passion with others. Olivia certainly had non-negotiables regarding her birthday party, one being that the theme would be all things unicorn. Just like Olivia, it is critical that we know exactly what our banner says so that it can become the mantra which moves our school's forward. Memorize it. Expect it. Model it. And most importantly, live it.

Wave Your Banner with Pride

To say that Olivia waved her banner with pride would be an understatement. She waved her birthday banner in the classroom. She waved it at lunch. She waved it at PE. She even waved it while the girls chatted in the bathroom.

How can your school wave the banner in a way that more effectively impacts kids? Teachers? Parents? Community members?

Let Others Carry the Banner for You

Olivia wasn't the only one carrying her birthday banner. Not only were kids carrying it with her, but they were also wearing it. Additionally, her birthday party was the topic of discussion at the teacher's lunch table. When the big day finally arrived, she had numerous teachers stop by to wish her a happy birthday. For an entire week, Olivia's birthday party was the hot topic.

What are parents and the community saying about your school? Do you give them a reason to want to talk about it? How can you cultivate a community where outsiders are carrying your school's banner for you?

Create experiences in your school that leave people begging for more. Be an Olivia and carry the banner in a way that multiplies.

Culture Builders

1. Drive Thru Parade - The week before school starts, have your bus drivers help you develop a route so that the entire faculty and staff can conduct a drive-by parade through a central part of your school's community. Advertise it on social media and suggest specific spots that families can drive to if you aren't driving by their house.

When we did this at Cedar Hill, we called our local radio station and had them play a specific playlist of songs so that everyone could sing and dance to the same music. Word of the parade traveled beyond our school family, and many community members, young and old, joined us for the parade as well. This is the perfect way to wave your school's banner with pride as you kick off the school year.

Additionally, you can also do what I like to call a "reverse parade". During the Covid-19 Pandemic, we wanted to find a way to honor our teachers during Teacher Appreciation Week, but due to social distancing, we were having a difficult time figuring out how to make it happen. We hosted a reverse parade in our car rider line where our families were invited to drive by to celebrate our teachers. In two hours' time, hundreds of cars drove by. Kids stood in the sunroof of decorated cars holding posters and gifts ready to toss to their teachers! The beautiful thing about a reverse parade is that it gives your community the opportunity to carry the banner for you. I'm convinced our school culture's positivity level doubled that day.

2. Engage Community Members - Do you have student ambassadors or peer helpers in your school? Is there a process in how you go about selecting these ambassadors? Consider inviting community members to be part of it.

Good grades and filling out a resume are the first steps, but our soft skills are what makes us employable. Both factors should be considered when selecting student ambassadors. Have your students go through an application and interview process during which they have to model their soft skills in real time. During the interview process, students can travel to different stations, with a community member at each station, rating every child and providing feedback.

Station Examples:

1. Have the kids introduce themselves to a community member. Did they offer a handshake? Did they exude confidence? Were they able to carry the conversation?
2. Have the kids try out to be the morning greeters in the carline and as the kids exit the buses. Do they greet everyone in sight? Are they excited about the school day?
3. Create a scenario where the applicant greets a new student and takes him/her on a tour of the school. Do they make the new student feel comfortable? How do they carry the banner when they talk about the school and everything it has to offer?
4. Sometimes, we are faced with situations that catch us off guard and we have to rely on strong soft skills to get us through it. Create a scenario where the community member has proudly made some baked good items, but unfortunately, the community member is unaware of how terrible they taste. How do the students maintain composure?

Community members will love being part of an event like this. They will leave the event carrying your school's banner, excited about the things you're doing to shape the future generation. Additionally, this is a great way to make kids aware of how important it is for them to carry the banner for your school. Eventually, maybe you can make this a school wide competition rather than limiting it to student ambassadors, but my advice would be to start small. Go slow first to go fast later.

3. "Meet the Teacher" Home Visits - In many schools, students find out who their teacher is by driving to the school to see the class lists hung on the door. While there is nothing wrong with this process, why not take the opportunity to make this moment a more exciting experience for everyone? Have the teachers travel to each of their new students' homes to meet them. Teachers can deliver a yard sign with the school's logo on it and take each child's picture for the upcoming school year.

This is a great way to kick off home visits for the school year if it's something you haven't been comfortable with in the past. Not only will this give you a head start in being aware of each child's circumstances, but it also creates the opportunity to build a positive relationship with every child. Carry the banner by showing how invested you are.

Reflection Questions

1. Reflect on the *Mindset Management Quadrant* near the beginning of this chapter. What is an area in which you need to pull yourself together and prioritize to maximize your impact?

2. If your school's community only knew about your school based on how you present yourself, what would its reputation be?

3. When your coworkers begin to feel weary or discouraged, do you enable or empower them?

4. How can your school wave the banner in a way that more effectively impacts students? Teachers? Parents? Community members?

5. What are parents and the community saying about your school? How can you cultivate a community where outsiders are carrying your school's banner for you?

CHAPTER 5

Core Principle 4: Be a Merchant of Hope

Welcome to Holland

Near the beginning of this book, I shared with you my unexpected roadblock in life: infertility. We have all landed in places in life that fill us with shock and sadness. Perhaps you have heard of the popular essay, Welcome to Holland, written by Emily Perl Kingsley (Kingsley, 1987). In this powerful essay, Kingsley writes about raising a child with a disability. The purpose of her essay is to help others who have not shared this same experience imagine how it would feel so they can fill themselves with compassion and empathy. As you read this, I want you to reflect on whatever moment you had in life that landed you in a world of undesired circumstances.

Being an expectant mother is like planning your perfect vacation trip to Italy. You purchase travel books and plan a detailed itinerary as you imagine the incredible places you have always dreamed of seeing—The Coliseum, the Tuscan hill towns, riding the gondolas in Venice. You even learn some useful Italian phrases. Months pass by and your excitement grows as you eagerly anticipate your dream vacation. Finally, it is time to pack your bags and board the plane to Italy.

Hours pass by, the plane descends to land and the captain announces over the speaker, "Welcome to Holland."

"Wait, what? Holland?" you say. "I don't know anything about Holland. I am supposed to be in Italy. Italy is what I have always planned for. For my entire life, I have longed to travel to Italy."

In the blink of an eye, there has been a change in the flight plan. You've landed in Holland, and you are there to stay. You are filled with shock, sadness, and disappointment, but amidst the emotional pain, you quickly realize that Holland is not a horrible, disgusting, dirty place. It is just a different place. Holland is slower paced and less flamboyant than Italy, but after you've resided there for a while, you catch your breath, your feet land on the ground, you look around.... and you begin to notice that Holland has windmills...and Holland has tulips. Holland even has Rembrandts. But everyone you know is busy coming and going from Italy... and they're all bragging about what a wonderful time they had there (Kingsley, 1987).

Yes, you would have loved to have traveled to Italy too. "That is where I was supposed to go. That was always my plan, too." For the rest of your life, you will wonder about the experience you missed, about the dreams you had hoped for. The grief of losing this dream will never fully go away. However, if we spend our life dwelling and mourning over not going to Italy, we will miss out on soaking up the wonderful and special things about Holland.

So now I ask you, what is your Holland? A diagnosis? A sudden career change? Maybe you have lost someone near and dear to you and you've found your plane has landed among the tulips.

It is in our hardships that we can reach out with what we have, even if it is with an unsteady hand, to help someone else. Don't be afraid to share your personal Holland story. When we share our stories about landing in Holland, we bring hope to the person who has not yet made it to the other side of their circumstances.

When you reach your Holland in life, there is always a merchant of hope waiting on you. Mine was Avery's birth mother. What many people don't realize about adoption is that it begins with brokenness. In the beginning, adoption is filled with sadness and trauma and darkness, but we only see the joy on social media. Avery's birth mother did not want to give Avery up, but she did it because she loved her enough to choose a different pathway for her. Saying goodbye to her was the hardest and most heart-wrenching thing I have ever seen and probably will ever witness. The selflessness she showed in that moment of sacrifice changed my life. In that moment of sacrifice, Avery was given the gift of a new beginning, and our emptiness was immediately filled when we were entrusted with one of God's most precious and eternal souls. All in the same moment of saying goodbye to her birth mother, we witnessed trauma and healing, heartbreak and joy, and broken and mended hearts. Birth mothers create a beautiful beginning for the child, for themselves, and for the adoptive family—a fresh start. But by doing that, they take on all the pain and heartbreak. They are the beginning in ending a broken situation. Avery's birth mother taught me some of life's greatest lessons, and because of her, I have an enriched understanding of true selflessness and sacrifice. Witnessing her example of unconditional love has changed my life because Avery's birth mother chose us. She redirected my own pathway by giving me the gift of motherhood. I will always look back at what seemed like the emptiest time of my life and see how God filled it with His glory when He sent Avery's birth mother to be my merchant of hope.

The fourth and final core principle when creating and maintaining a "culturized" school is that every staff member in the building must aspire to be a merchant of hope for the kids they serve. Oftentimes, being a merchant of hope to someone else does more for you than it does for the person who was helped because when we desire to help others, we fill ourselves with selflessness and service. As educators, we have the advantage to use our own experiences to connect with a child. It's not about us, ever. It's about shaping kids' futures. Skepticism shatters when we seek to see the beauty in a broken situation. When you are broken, and you are so clouded and can't see the light at the end of the tunnel, look for the opportunity you're not yet seeing, the chance to multiply excellence by being a merchant of hope for a student. Take time to heal, look for the beauty, and just take it one day at a time.

Whatever It Takes

Brayden's Story

"Brayden, you haven't completed any of your assignments today."

"Brayden, please keep your hands to yourself."

"Brayden, it's not polite to throw food in the lunchroom."

Brayden was a 2nd grader who was new to our school. It was the first month of school, and his teacher, Mrs. Reece was doing everything she could to mold and shape him to be successful, but she was having very little success. Brayden couldn't slow his mind down enough to listen to instructions. He had zero desire to learn and refused to do his work. His impulsive outbursts created chaos wherever he went. Every day with Brayden was a challenge.

One day, Mrs. Reece pulled me aside in the hallway to tell me about the tough morning Brayden was having. I stood there and listened, and before I could respond, she said these powerful words: "I don't want him to be punished. He just needs a break, a reset. I'm just trying to figure out how to help him in my own classroom."

If only we could all have a heart as big as Mrs. Reece's.

I wish I could say that we solved all of Brayden's problems that day, but we didn't. Why? Because we hadn't yet tapped into Brayden's true interference. Remember, kids aren't bad for the sake of being bad. There is always an underlying cause.

Weeks went by, and Mrs. Reece continued to pour herself into Brayden. Her expectations of him never wavered; however, she began to take note of strange observations about Brayden that sent her some red flags. Every morning, she began asking him questions to better understand his reality so she could meet his needs.

"Brayden, what did you eat for dinner last night?"

"Brayden, whose house did you sleep at last night?"

"Brayden, I noticed your shoes have holes in them. Do you have any other tennis shoes at home?"

Brayden's answers began to open her eyes to see that there were much bigger problems in his life, far beyond the fact that he had trouble achieving success at school. His physiological needs weren't being met, the safety in his home was unsteady, and he lacked a sense of connection with others. When this realization came to fruition, we had a clear understanding of why we were having trouble reaching him.

Brayden had never been taught a proper way to act, and his shattered homelife sent his mind into a constant tailspin. Over the next few months, Mrs. Reece bent over backwards to help Brayden reach success.

When Brayden had trouble completing his work, she let him wear special headphones and listen to The Lion King soundtrack. Why? Because she learned that he focused better when he listened to music, and The Lion King was his favorite movie.

When he walked into her classroom with bloodshot eyes because he didn't sleep the night before, she provided a place for him to rest so he could reach his potential the rest of the day.

When he arrived at school looking lethargic, she asked him what he wanted to eat, because she knew that was a telltale sign he hadn't eaten dinner the night before.

When Brayden became over-stimulated in the classroom, she gave him the gift of a sensory break to help him slow down his mind.

When Brayden reached his boiling point and was too young to understand why, she asked if I could help him de-escalate in my office.

Every day with Brayden was a challenge. Every single day. But not one time did Mrs. Reece lose her patience. Not one time did she tell him he knew better. Not one time did she stop brainstorming out-of-the-box ideas to help him reach success. Mrs. Reece was relentless, and she proved she will do whatever it takes to go to bat for a child.

At the end of the school year, Brayden developed a love of reading and reached proficiency on all the standard requirements for his grade level. You see, Brayden's potential was inside of him all along. But when kids like Brayden are born in Holland, they don't know how to find beauty when it is the only world they know. It is our job, as teachers, to grow flowers inside of their innocent minds so that beauty may be revealed. Just like Mrs. Reece, it is our job to become merchants of hope.

Mid-year, Mrs. Reece began going on weekly home visits to Brayden's home. She bought groceries for the family. She brought the kids special treats. When she read Brayden books, his teenage sister sat beside her to listen as well. When the school year ended, Mrs. Reece continued to visit Brayden's family in the summer. She became a beautiful example to Brayden's mom of what stability, selflessness and service looks like. Brayden's entire family fell in love with his merchant of hope.

The greatest way to find your purpose as an educator is to lose yourself in the service of others. When kids are struggling, seek out the interference. See their pain and meet them with compassion. Then reach out with service and selflessness. This is what it means to be a merchant of hope. It's not about us. It's about kids.

IT'S NOT ABOUT US.

IT'S ABOUT KIDS.

Say this to yourself over and over again until this mentality becomes ingrained inside of you. When we allow selfless seeds to take root in the garden of our hearts, that is when we will become merchants of hope to kids. That is when we are in the business of changing lives. That is when we will multiply excellence.

Stop Judging Parents

Chloe.

The girl who wasn't afraid to cuss or deck another student out if they rubbed her the wrong way. The girl who was my most frequent flyer for office referrals. The girl who taught me the most about compassion, patience, perseverance, and hope.

You already know from Chapter 3 that my relationship with Chloe was rocky in the beginning, but in time, our adoration and respect for one another grew by leaps and bounds. In Chapter 1, you learned that her mother was the root cause behind Chloe's outbursts because she had modeled that lashing out was the only way to respond to conflict.

I was chewed out more times by Chloe's mother in the first few months of meeting her than I have been by any other parents combined in my career. She had no reservations in showing up at the school unannounced to blast me, or somebody else for something we had supposedly done.

"Mrs. Paschall, Ms. Stark is in the front office and wants to talk to you."

Every time I heard those words, I felt exasperated. Oh, how I dreaded my interactions with Ms. Stark!

One day after school, Chloe refused to get off the bus to walk inside her house. After many failed attempts, the bus driver eventually brought Chloe back to the school. Her mother caught wind of this before I could even make it to the front office and asked our receptionist to deliver this message to me.

"You tell Mrs. Paschall that she can call the cops to come and pick Chloe up! I'm not coming up there to get her. I can't leave work! I'm so sick of Chloe's crap!"

When her mother finally realized she had no other choice, she drove to the school and burst into my office in a rage, ready to blow a gasket. I spent the first few minutes listening, and then stated this response:

"Ms. Stark, I understand that you are very upset with Chloe right now. And I understand you're upset with me. But you're currently in a state that has me feeling very uncomfortable with allowing Chloe to get in the car to go home with you. I want to help you, and I want to help Chloe. Help me understand what has you the most upset."

Immediately, the tears began to flow.

"Mrs. Paschall, I can't do this anymore. I can't handle raising these five kids by myself. I can't handle Chloe's smart mouth. I'm behind on paying my bills. I don't have enough money for groceries. I am exhausted. I am completely exhausted, and I am on the verge of having a nervous breakdown."

It was the first time Ms. Stark let her walls down and faced her reality in front of me. Finally, she had opened her window of receptivity for help. I spent the next hour listening to her situation and offering advice. My previous feelings of exasperation were quickly being replaced with compassion. From that day forward, staff members began making weekly home visits to the Stark house, not just to see the kids, but because Ms. Stark also needed a champion. When things began to escalate in the home, the mother reached a point where she felt comfortable enough to contact one of us for support.

During one of my home visits, the mother and I sat on the porch making small talk, and the conversation led to her opening up about how she had never had any stability in her own life. She grew up in a broken home, filled with drugs and alcohol. Men were in and out of her mom's life. Tears streamed down her face as she talked about how disappointed she was in herself for not breaking the cycle for her own kids.

"I never had a positive experience in school. Ever! Y'all are a first for me, that's for sure. You're different, Mrs. Paschall."

At that moment, I was filled with so much guilt for pre-judging Ms. Stark earlier in the year. Truth is, Ms. Stark loved her kids, and she wanted to be a good mom to them. Additionally, she wanted to reach her own personal success. But the reality was that she hadn't yet found her own merchant of hope in life to inspire her to redirect her own pathway.

After the day Chloe refused to get off the bus, Ms. Stark and my relationship was vastly different. If Chloe got in trouble at school, Ms. Stark maintained her composure and respected whatever action step was taken. When I visited her house each week, she welcomed me with open arms. When I offered advice on parenting, she humbly and openly accepted it. Why? Because she didn't feel judged. She felt supported.

It is difficult for us to meet the pain of others and not compare it to our own, or worse, judge them. We see the choices others make and almost instinctively compare them to our own choices. How wrong this mentality is. Merchants of hope are filled with service and selflessness. This leaves no room for judgmental thoughts. See their brokenness and pain and meet it with love and compassion.

I wish I could tell you there is a beautiful outcome to this story, but nothing has a quick fix. We are in the trenches every single day. All hands are on deck as we work to carry this family through the hardships of life, and we are committed to do so as long as it is within our control. Every day, we wake up and make the choice to strive to be the Stark family's merchants of hope.

At the end of the day, our number one responsibility is to do what is best for kids, but don't give up on the parents too quickly. The number one goal should always be to keep families together. Sometimes championing kids means also championing parents. Stop judging parents, meet them with compassion, and help them unbecome whatever is hindering them from championing their own child. Be the merchant of hope who multiplies excellence in the entire family.

Reflect, Reboot, Restore

Teachers hold the greatest influence in reaching a child at school, and it's critical we are consistently pouring into them so they can become their best self in the classroom. In every classroom, at every school, we want nothing but the very best for every student. The best way we can do this is by providing teachers the opportunity to reflect, reboot, and restore themselves each year as they work to master their craft.

Whatever role you are in, take a moment to reflect on the following questions. If you revisit these questions year after year, you will find it interesting to see how your answers change as you grow yourself.

1. On a scale of 1-10, how close are you to reaching your ideal of where you aspire to be in your current role? Why?

_____

_____

_____

2. Which students did you make a deep connection with this year and why? How did you do this?

_____

_____

_____

3. Which students did you have a difficult time connecting with? What did you do about it?

_____

_____

_____

4. Reflect on your data for the school year. What percentage of students exceeded academically? Why did they excel?

    _____

    _____

    _____

5. Think about your students who didn't excel academically? Why was this the case?

    _____

    _____

    _____

6. If your data isn't where you want them to be, what are your thoughts and beliefs about being able to change it?

    _____

    _____

    _____

7. Develop an action plan listing what you are going to do to move yourself forward to being exemplary. Include how you will measure your growth, as well as how you will receive support from your supervisor(s), instructional coach, colleagues and/or other professional connections.

    _____

    _____

    _____

_____

_____

_____

_____

_____

_____

_____

_____

What did you learn about yourself? Were any questions difficult for you to answer? Think about Nick Saban, who many would consider to be the greatest college football coach of all time. Do you think he is ever where he wants to be? Of course not. That is why he is the multi-million-dollar coach. Without reflection, there is no growth. As educators, it is important that we slow down and take time to deeply reflect on our level of impact. This is the only way we can truly move ourselves forward.

> "We do not learn from experience.
> We learn from reflecting on experience."
> John Dewey

Be a merchant of hope to kids.
Be a merchant of hope to parents.
Lastly, we must be merchants of hope to each other.
Administrators, it is your job to lead teachers to restore themselves until they reach exemplary status in the classroom. Every teacher wants to be great. Every teacher is teachable. Every teacher needs a leader who is willing to initiate this restoration process.

At the beginning of each summer, after you've all had a few days to relax your minds, schedule a meeting with your newer teachers so that you can take them on a reflection journey with the seven previous questions. It is important that you ask these questions in person so that it creates the opportunity for open dialogue.

"We want nothing but 10's at our school: every classroom ideal, high performing and exemplary. And it is my job to support you and help you get yourself there—and do it quickly."

Tell them this. It is critical that you set the bar high and tell them you believe they can become a 10. Be their merchant of hope by leading them to build their fullest capacity so that they can make the greatest possible difference in kids' lives. There is no greater feeling than to confidently know you're giving your best so that others can become their best.

While there is certainly a time and a place for classroom evaluations, I want to make a clear distinction between the two. If we only tell teachers what they did well or what they need to work on after a snapshot lesson, that is not enough. It takes these deeper conversations, not just a post observation conference, to lead teachers to restore themselves. This isn't a checkbox. This is time to get them to reflect. Asking these questions will help determine if a teacher has a growth mindset. You cannot get to the heart of their personal belief system and the relationships they form with kids during an observation reflection.

The most important part of this meeting is that you end it by asking them to create their own action plan that states how they plan to move themselves forward to becoming exemplary the following school year. Do not complete this task for them. Remember, self-empowerment is not something we feel. It is something we do. Our sense of empowerment is a reflection of the increased self-confidence that derives from our experience of knowing that what we are doing is making a difference. When they send the action plan to you, provide feedback and look for two important things:

1. Did they include in this action plan what they want support to look like from the instructional coach, as well as you, the administrator? This support should include them expecting classroom observation and feedback.

2. Did they include how they will receive support from their colleagues? An action plan should always include collaboration.

> Empowered teachers create a chain reaction of influence all around them. Empowered teachers become merchants of hope. Empowered teachers multiply excellence.

Teachers need to hear us say we believe they can become a 10. There is no better way to model how we want them to become merchants of hope for kids. They need to know that you believe that they can one day fly. Be their merchant of hope by leading them to a place of self-empowerment.

Why? Because: empowered teachers create a chain reaction of influence all around them. Empowered teachers become merchants of hope. Empowered teachers multiply excellence.

Make Stepping Stones Out of Stumbling Blocks

March 26, 2020

"Students, Parents, and Guardians,

Due to the rising health concerns with COVID-19, a state of emergency has been declared in our state. Our governor and state superintendent have decided to close school buildings for the rest of the year...

...In the coming days, we will reach out to you on all communication platforms outlining the plans to carry out school from home for the rest of the 2019-2020 school year..."

I'll never forget the crushing feeling that came over me when I received this letter from the Superintendent in my school district. For weeks, schools across the nation received this devastating news. Hearing and reading these words felt like a punch straight to the gut. Educators across the country were shaken to the core as we digested all of the things that had been left undone. We still had so much to teach, so many hugs to give, and so many little hearts and minds to mold.

Suddenly, there had been a change in our flight plans.

Suddenly, we weren't destined for Italy anymore.

Suddenly, we had all landed in Holland, and we were there to stay.

The day we received the news about schools closing, I received endless texts and phone calls from teachers.

"What now?"

"How are we going to make sure our students are fed?"

*"I can't even wrap my brain around this. So many of my students **need** to be at school to escape their reality."*

"How am I supposed to stay connected to Logan to make sure he is doing ok?"

"So, what now, Mrs. Paschall?!"

Their spirits were shattered. My spirit was shattered. That night, I'm not sure I even slept two hours.

Defeat. Shock. Confusion. Fear. Sadness.

These are just a few emotions that I was consumed with that night. I'm sure you can relate if you've faced any sort of tragedy in your school. After I had some time to let our new reality sink in, I finally faced the question I had been asked by our teachers time and time again.

"So, what now?"

"The only difference between a stumbling block
and a stepping stone is how you use them."

Unknown

We had been faced with a stumbling block. I didn't have the answers. No one did. But there were three things I did know:

1. Together, we could find a way to turn that stumbling block into a stepping stone.
2. We had to find a way to stay connected with our students.
3. Teachers will go above and beyond to serve as merchants of hope for kids. Sometimes, they just need permission to jump out of the nest and fly.

All it took on my part was a simple text message suggesting that we meet and collaborate. That Saturday night, many members of our faculty met to work out a plan. Over the next two months, our teachers went above and beyond to meet kids' needs.

Each week, one of our bus drivers and a resource teacher created directed drawing videos and took the kids on virtual field trips to their farm, all via social media. Teachers became pen pals with their students via email. Teachers mailed handwritten letters to the kids. Many of our teachers surprised the kids with a special treat every Friday to celebrate #FaceLiftFridays, just to give their students a reason to smile and feel loved.

When a student struggled to master an academic skill, our teachers didn't hesitate to take it to the house and teach them through the window. When several of our broken families were struggling with mental health because school was their only outlet, our PE coach visited them and brought their favorite PE game to play with them. When Mother's Day rolled around, one of our teachers invited her students over, one small group at a time and marked x's in her driveway so the kids could still create a Mother's Day present.

1,018.

1,018 home visits our teachers went on between March 26th and the last day of school.

1,018 reminders of our WHY.

1,018 reminders why face-to-face learning is hands down better than virtual learning.

> Our mantra became, "Connection before content." Always. In that order. But we didn't fall prey to thinking content didn't matter.
>
>

Our mantra became, "Connection before content." Always. In that order. But we didn't fall prey to thinking content didn't matter. Connection is the gateway to learning. And learning is what diverts kids' pathways and futures.

Our teachers' hearts were exploding with love and it was a beautiful thing to see during this difficult time. They were willing to do whatever it took to meet their kids' needs in their own, unique way. The best part? They chose to find beauty in Holland. Suddenly landing in Holland was one of the best things that could have ever happened to us. Cedar Hill Elementary will never be the same as a result of COVID-19.

A school's true culture is illuminated when tragedy hits. How do you respond to this? Do you allow circumstances to define your students' present and future? Or do you do whatever it takes to rise above them? Kids don't need us to be merchants of hope during the easy times. It is in the darkest moments that they need their merchant of hope to selflessly carry them through the storm.

When our school lands in Holland, we must always be ready to think outside the box so that we can continue to be merchants of hope for kids. Skepticism shatters when we seek to see the beauty in a broken situation. Leaders don't view stumbling blocks as a closed door. They view them as an opportunity to build culture.

My challenge for you is this: Don't allow circumstances to dictate your journey, Instead, let them determine your starting point. Circumstances don't make or break a school's culture, they reveal it. When stumbling blocks get in your way, look at them as stepping stones. In the midst of hardship, there are always ways to multiply excellence. Never stop looking for opportunities to become someone else's merchant of hope.

Culture Builders

1. Visit Teachers' Homes - One of the most common questions I get asked by other administrators is, "How do I get teacher buy-in when trying to implement something new?" What we really want is for teachers to take ownership. "Buy-in" is rooted in compliance, while "ownership" is rooted in intrinsic motivation and commitment. Sometimes teachers need to experience something firsthand to feel the impact it can make on a child. Home visits are essential in a "culturized" school, but they are uncomfortable for teachers at first, which hinders them from taking ownership of the process. Have your admin team (as well as a few parents, if needed) help you deliver a special gift to every staff member right at their own doorstep. You could deliver a yard sign, a newly designed school shirt, or a surprise lunch. The ideas are endless. What's important is that you make teachers feel appreciated and allow them to experience what it feels like for someone to go out of their way to visit them at their own home. When teachers understand the value of implementing a new process, they are more likely to take ownership. And when that happens, the new process is much more likely to stick and become embedded into your culture.

2. Community Involvement - It's important for kids to see us outside of school. Look for opportunities to be involved in their community, such as attending little league games, community festivals, or even church services. When kids see your interest and investment in them outside your classroom, they will begin to see how valuable their time is with you inside the classroom. Additionally, this establishes new opportunities to build connections with kids. For those kids who are harder to reach, you can talk about the event together which becomes the springboard to building deeper relationships. Involving yourself in the community gives you a bridge between their life and yours.

3. Make Mornings Fun - While we may not have control over what kids face before they arrive at school each day, we do have control over redirecting the course of their day. How can you find a way to collectively start every child's school day on a positive note?

Each day at Cedar Hill, our school custodians and I stand in a central location and play upbeat music so that we can excitedly greet every student in our school. Many of the kids drop their backpacks and take a few minutes to dance and sing with us. Teachers and substitute teachers also enjoy coming down to become part of the excitement. School is an exciting place to be. Why not make the first moments of every kid's school day joyful and fun?

We must find ways to become merchants of hope to kids both individually and collectively. The beauty of this morning tradition is that our custodians are given a special time to bond with the kids. Our custodians make a wonderfully positive impact on our school's culture.

Your school's support staff plays an important role in contributing to the culture of your school. Be sure that you are intentional about providing opportunities for them to build relationships with kids.

Reflection Questions

1. Think of the most difficult student you have ever dealt with. How would you handle the situation differently now?

2. What practices do you need to put into place so that you can connect with potentially difficult parents instead of having conflicts with them?

3. Think back to a time in your life or career where stumbling blocks were placed in your path. How did you convert them to stepping stones?

CHAPTER 6

Multiply Excellence

The person who multiplies excellence in others is the leader. Regardless of our role, we should be living and leading in a way that creates a ripple effect of excellence in others.

Think about the people you are surrounded by each day. Is this happening? Think about the people you're teaching and leading. Are you teaching and leading in a way that multiplies excellence? Over the years, I have come to the realization that there is a difference between being an influencer and a multiplier. We influence kids when we deliver engaging lessons which excite them about learning. We often Influence others to become better educators in a faculty meeting, during professional development, and through blog posts. If 100 people in a room can be influenced, this is a great start. But in all of these situations, you influence people broadly and from afar. If we want to become change agents in education, we've got to be sure we are multiplying excellence, and to do this, we must be up close and personal. It begins with relationships.

Remember Mr. Wade from Chapter 1, the person who sparked my passion for education? My first interaction with Mr. Wade was when he was my professor for a course about Classroom Management. He is the first person who caused me to feel emotion about my future career. He is also the person who helped me to understand that relationships are the gateway to a kid's heart. And when we are passionate about reaching kids' hearts, they desire to learn from us, and *then* we can teach them. When Mr. Wade was my college professor, he

> If we want to become change agents in education, we've got to be sure we are multiplying excellence, and to do this, we must be up close and personal. It begins with relationships.
>
> ~

had a great deal of influence in shaping my core beliefs about education. But during the time he was my professor, I was one of many students in the room being influenced by his genuine and infectious spirit. It wasn't until Mr. Wade hired me to be his After School Care Director that I was able to get to know him on a personal level. That is when he began to multiply excellence within me.

"Emily, do you realize how special you are? You have so many gifts, so many things to offer in the world of education. Not only do you have the brains, but you also have the people skills. And most importantly, you have the heart for kids. The sky's the limit for you, my friend. I cannot wait to see how your career takes off."

These are the words Mr. Wade would say to me when I was a college student and working part time in his school. At the time, I was just an immature kid who was ready to graduate college. I hadn't even begun to think about where I could end up 10, 20, or 30 years down the road. But Mr. Wade did. Because of the time he invested in building a relationship with me, he has made the greatest impact in accelerating my career pathway. Why? Because at a youthful 20 years of age, he saw a potential in me I didn't yet know existed. He believed in me, and he told me over and over again about what he saw in me until I started to believe it about myself. To this day, Mr. Wade continues to impact my life. I cherish the days we get to catch up over the phone and in person.

This book is meant to help you become a better teacher and leader—students, for teachers, and for parents. My hope is that you don't read or listen to this book just to receive, but to multiply. How will you put these ideas into practice in your own life? How will you multiply this learning in others? Because if it is stopping with us, we are missing the whole point. Learning about leadership and excellence should not stop with us. It should spread through us.

Level up by shifting your mentality from being one who influences others to one who multiplies excellence in others.

As you actively make this shift, commit to these five ways to improve yourself so that you can multiply excellence in others.

1. Love What You Do - Let it be written all over your face that you love what you *get* to do each day. Carry the banner for your school by loving your school and your chosen profession. Greet your coworkers and students with excitement. Deliver lessons that leave kids begging for more. Give grace when others make mistakes. Always, always, always choose joy. We work in the kid business. You must leave your personal stresses in the car when you arrive at school each day. We can't let our personal lives interfere with our mission in education. Love what you do and make it so obvious that it multiplies the same level of excitement in others.

2. Nurture Relationships - Relationships are the first step in igniting a change within someone else. Reflect on your connection with the people in your building. When excellence multiplies, it stems from a firmly rooted relationship. Are you continuously nurturing these relation-ships? Spend time getting to know your coworkers, students, and parents. When someone knows how much you care, then they will desire to learn from you. Water them often and watch them grow.

3. Be Tenacious - I am to the point where I believe that every excuse we make for why kids can't achieve is invalid. The reality is that we just haven't yet discovered the true interference or how to help them overcome it. Every child in America is depending on us to aid them in paving their pathway toward success. This leaves zero room for excuses and zero room for giving up when plan A, B, and C don't work. Be tenacious in your pursuit for championing all kids. Lead others to become their best self so they can be the best for kids. In order to champion for kids, we also have to champion for teachers. Celebrate them, embrace difficult conversations, and stay in the trenches as you help them grow.

4. Seek Excellence - We're never really finished reaching excellence. Education is ever-changing, so our expectation of excellence should be also. Grow your network. Read. Step outside the four walls of your school. Hire for excellence. Seek out people who will tell it to you straight, regardless of whether you want to hear it. If you want to multiply excellence in others, you've got to be hungry for excelling yourself.

5. Take Risks - We must be willing to take risks for two reasons. The first reason is that taking risks is how we innovate and make positive changes. Risk-taking steers us away from the "this is the way we have always done it" mentality. The second reason is because our students and staff need to see how we handle ourselves when risk taking goes poorly. How do we respond? How do we overcome it? What adjustments do we need to make? We all fall down, but just because we have fallen doesn't mean we've failed. We fail when we don't choose to stand back up. We must model this for our students and staff. Taking risk makes you stronger and fosters risk-taking in those around you. Boldly go forward.

There is joy to be found in multiplying excellence in others because it gives us a purpose—to fulfill the mission we've been called to do—to help all kids become the best version of themselves. This is the joy of teaching, when we pour ourselves into others. As we find that purpose, we find fulfillment.

> We all fall down, but just because we have fallen doesn't mean we've failed. We fail when we don't choose to stand back up.

An educator's job is too important to just be mediocre. None of us chose teaching to be average. We must remember our why each and every day so that we can continuously rise above the status quo mentality.

Bring your best, every day, and most importantly, multiply excellence in others. Together, let's leave our mark on this generation of kids that can never be erased.

References

Bearden, K. (2018). *Talk to Me: Find the right words to inspire, encourage and get things done: 6 principles of effective communication*. San Diego, CA: Dave Burgess Consulting, Incorporated.

Block, P. (2000). *Flawless consulting: A Guide to Getting Your Expertise Used*. San Francisco, California: Pfeiffer.

Casas, J. (2017). *Culturize: Every student, every day, whatever it takes*. San Diego, CA: Dave Burgess Consulting, Incorporated.

Casas, J. (2019, July 29). *Culturize: Every Student. Every Day. Whatever It Takes*. Lecture presented at LCS Leadership Conference in Calhoun Community College, Athens.

Esdal, L. (2019, February 28). Why Teachers Leave: What the Data Say [Web log post]. Retrieved March 6, 2019, from https://www.educationevolving.org/blog/2019/02/why-teachers-leave-what-data-say

Good, A. (2016, March 25). Crestline's Jerome Lewis named finalist in national Janitor of the Year contest. Retrieved June 17, 2020, from https://www.alabamanewscenter.com/2016/03/28/crestlines-jerome-lewis-named-finalist-national-janitor-year-contest/

Kingsley, E. P. (2001). Welcome to Holland. Contact, 136(1), 14–14. https://doi.org/10.1080/13520806.2001.11758925

Maslow, A. H. (2018). *Theory of human motivation*. S.l.: Wilder Publications.

Maslow, A. H. (n.d.). Abraham Maslow Quotes. Retrieved July 03, 2020, from https://www.brainyquote.com/quotes/abraham_maslow_106490

Maxwell, J. C. (2005). *Developing the leaders around you.* Nashville, TN: Nelson Business.

Merriam-Webster. (n.d.). Excellence. In *Merriam-Webster.com dictionary.* Retrieved July 6, 2020, from https://www.merriam-webster.com/dictionary/excellence

Nesloney, T., & Welcome, A. (2016). *Kids deserve it!: Pushing boundaries and challenging conventional thinking* (p. 135). San Diego, CA: Dave Burgess Consulting.

Twitter.com. 2017. Twitter. [online] Available at: <https://twitter.com/mraspinall/status/932036662653267968/photo/1> [Accessed 13 July 2020].

Acknowledgements

To my family: My appreciation and love for you all is abounding. Jared, thank you for your unwavering support in all steps of life and for encouraging me to pursue my dreams. Thank you to my parents for teaching me through example about endless love and service. And to my daughter Avery, who lights up every room she walks into—you have taught me more about joy in your little life than I have learned in all of mine! I love you all.

To my cheerleaders: A tremendous thank you to Allison Usery, Casie Barksdale, and Karen Brown. I am grateful to call you my friends and mentors. Thank you for believing in me, for having my back, and for patiently listening to me work through my thoughts while I was writing this book. And to Zac McCray, thank you for being my sounding board and supporting me on this journey.

To Adam Welcome: Thank you for pushing me to take the leap in social media by kicking off the #ElemAPNetwork. Your encouragement and belief in me have truly changed my life.

To Jimmy Casas and Jeff Zoul: This book would have never happened without the two of you. Thank you for your vision, for believing in me, and for inspiring me to share my passion with others. Thank you for making a way for educators to share their voice so that together we can make a greater impact on the future of our world.

About the Author

E MILY PASCHALL has served as a teacher, district coach, school administrator, professional learning trainer, and motivational speaker.

Her passions lie in teaching, learning, and serving others. She leads a nationwide group of administrators through supportive social media sites with shared ideas, information, and motivation. She is best known for founding the #ElemAPNetwork where she offers various opportunities for administrators to experience a live exchange of best practices and fresh ideas. Her work is recognized around the world from educators who desire to learn how to create a climate and culture that promotes excellence.

Emily's innovative methods for driving student engagement, promoting academic rigor, and stimulating excitement about school has created a ripple effect in others across the country.

To book future speaking engagements, contact her at EmilyAPaschall@gmail com. You can also connect with her on Twitter, Instagram and Voxer: @EmilyAPaschall

More from ConnectEDD Publishing

Since 2015, ConnectEDD has worked to transform education by empowering educators to become better-equipped to teach, learn, and lead. What started as a small company designed to provide professional learning events for educators has grown to include a variety of services to help teachers and administrators address essential challenges. ConnectEDD offers instructional and leadership coaching, professional development workshops focusing on a variety of educational topics, a roster of nationally-recognized educator associates who possess hands-on knowledge and experience, educational conferences custom-designed to meet the specific needs of schools, districts, and state/national organizations, and ongoing, personalized support, both virtually and onsite. In 2020, ConnectEDD expanded to include publishing services designed to provide busy educators with books and resources consisting of practical information on a wide variety of teaching, learning, and leadership topics. Please visit us online at connecteddpublishing.com or contact us at:

info@connecteddpublishing.com

Recent Publications:

Live Your Excellence: Action Guide by Jimmy Casas

Culturize: Action Guide by Jimmy Casas

Daily Inspiration for Educators: Positive Thoughts for Every Day of the Year by Jimmy Casas

 ConnectEDD